Also by John P. Cann:
Counterinsurgency in Africa. The Portuguese Way of War 1961-74
Flight Plan Africa: Portuguese Airpower in Counterinsurgency 1961-1974
Brown Waters of Africa. Portuguese Riverine Warfare 1961-1974
A@W The Flechas. Insurgent Hunting in Eastern Angola, 1965-1974

Published by
Helion & Company Limited
26 Willow Road, Solihull, West Midlands,
B91 1UE, England
Tel. 0121 705 3393
Fax 0121 711 4075
Email: info@helion.co.uk
Website: www.helion.co.uk
Twitter: @helionbooks
Visit our blog http://blog.helion.co.uk/

Designed and typeset by Kerrin Cocks,
SA Publishing Services
kerrincocks@gmail.com
Cover design by Paul Hewitt,
Battlefield Design
www.battlefield-design.co.uk
Printed by Henry Ling Ltd, Dorchester
Dorset

Text © John P. Cann, 2016
Monochrome/color images and maps © as
individually credited

Cover: LDM 301 landing a section of DFE 13
on a *bolanha* in the Cacheu River.
(Source: Personal archive of Admiral Nuno
Vieira Matias)

ISBN 978-1-910777-64-0

British Library Cataloguing-in-Publication
Data.
A catalogue record for this book is available
from the British Library.

CONTENTS

GLOSSARY

ANC	African National Congress
Bapat	*Base de Patrulhas de Ganturé*, or Patrol Base Ganturé
CAOP	*Comando de Agrupamento Operacional Permanente*, or Permanent Operational Group Command
CDMG	*Comando de Defesa Martíma da Guiné*, or Maritme Defense Command of Guiné
CDMPA	*Comando da Defesa Marítima de Porto Amélia*, or Maritime Defense Command Porto Amélia
CF	*companhia de fuzileiros*, or company of fuzileiros
CNM	*Comando Naval de Moçambique*, or Naval Command Mozambique
COP	*Comando Operacional Permanente*, or Permanent Operational Command
DESTACMAR –CUANDO	*Destacamento de Marinha do Rio Cuando*, or Naval Detachment Cuando
DESTACMAR –CUITO	*Destacamento de Marinha do Rio Cuito*, or Naval Detachment Cuito
DFE	*destacamento de fuzileiros especiais*, or detachment of special fuzileiros
ELFG	*Esquadrilha de Lanchas de Fiscalização de Guiné*, or Patrol Launch Squadron Guiné
FNLA	*Frente Nacional de Libertação de Angola*, or National Front for the Liberation of Angola
FRELIMO	*Frente de Libertação de Moçambique*, or Front for the Liberation of Mozambique
FZ	*fuzileiros navais*, or naval fuzileiros
FZE	*fuzileiros especiais*, or special fuzileiros
GA	*grupo de assault*, or assault group
GRAE	*Governo da República de Angola no Exílo*, or Government of the Republic of Angola in Exile
LCA	landing craft assault
LCM	landing craft medium
LCT	landing craft tank
LD	*lancha de desembarque*, or landing craft
LDG	*lancha de desembarque grande*, or landing craft large
LDM	*lancha de desembarque média*, or landing craft medium
LDP	*lancha de desembarque pequena*, or landing craft small
LF	*lancha de fiscalização*, or patrol launch
LFG	*lancha de fiscalização grande*, or large patrol launch
LFP	*lancha de fiscalização pequena*, or small patrol launch
MPLA	*Movimento Popular de Libertação de Angola*, or Popular Movement for the Liberation of Angola
PAIGC	*Partido Africano da Independência da Guiné e Cabo Verde*, or African Party for the Independence of Guinea and Cape Verde
PAC	Pan African Congress
PTO	*preparação técnica operacional*, or operational technique preparation
RPG	rocket-propelled grenade
UNITA	*União Nacional para a Independência Total de Angola*, or National Union for the Total Independence of Angola
UPA	*Uniao das Populações de Angola*, or Union of Angolan Peoples
ZANU	Zimbabwe African National Union

INTRODUCTION

Between 1961 and 1974, Portugal faced the extremely ambitious task of conducting three simultaneous counterinsurgency campaigns in Guiné, Angola and Mozambique. It was at the time neither a wealthy nor a well-developed country. In fact, it was the least wealthy Western European nation by most standards of economic measure – thus for Portugal in 1961 to have mobilized an armed force, transported it many thousands of miles to its African colonies, established a sophisticated logistic infrastructure to support it, equipped it with special weapons and matériel, and trained it for a very specialized type of warfare was a remarkable achievement. It is made even more noteworthy by the fact that these tasks were accomplished without any previous experience, doctrine, or demonstrated competence in the field of either power projection or counterinsurgency warfare, and thus without the benefit of any instructors who were competent in these specialties. To put this last statement in perspective, other than periodic pacification efforts, Portugal had not fired a shot in anger in Africa since World War One, when Germany invaded Northern

Mozambique and Southern Angola.

The Portuguese defense establishment was quite familiar with the principles of counterinsurgency, was aware that its troops were not going to fight a classic conventional war and understood that forces had to be modified and adapted to the job at hand. There was substantial concern throughout the armed forces in undertaking what would be a wholesale and radical change in force structure and training, as it would affect all aspects of traditional tactics, techniques and procedures. It would very much disturb the status quo, and thus professional career paths. Nevertheless, Portugal proceeded to adapt its forces to a new way of war and created a force uniquely tailored to fight in this new struggle. It changed its forces to fit the war rather than trying to fight a war with the wrong forces.

One of the most noteworthy of these developments was the use of Special Forces to hunt the insurgents. Because of the vastness and the terrain variation of the battlefield, there was specialization within these forces. The fuzileiros, or Marines, were employed in the riverine environment – and our story begins with their reinstitution to support river security. In a riverine environment, security must be extended ashore along the riverbanks to control use of the river. Because roads in Africa are poor, rivers are the preferred avenue for moving cargo and people. They also provide references in a vast area devoid of landmarks and present barriers to be crossed, and Africa has many, many rivers. In the following pages we will explore just how the fuzileiros of the Portuguese Navy brought security to the riverine systems across the three theaters and examine their organization, employment and effectiveness in doing so.

CHAPTER 1
INTO AFRICA

Beginning in 1947 with the independence of India, Great Britain began the dissolution of its Empire. After two unsatisfactory colonial wars (one in Indochina and the other in Algeria), France dismantled its Empire. Portugal was now the remaining colonial power. Its position was very different from Britain and France in that it had been in Africa since the beginning of the 15th century – over four-and-a-half centuries – and longer by far than any other colonial power. It considered its overseas territories, known as the *ultramar*, an integral part of continental Portugal and refused to consider granting independence to them. Its commitment to their defense had its origins not only in their long-term ownership, but also in their economic promise and the inflexible African policy of Dr António Salazar, the Prime Minister. With the progressive decline of its trading position in the Indian Ocean beginning in 1578, the loss of its colony of Brazil in 1822 and the missed opportunity of a coast-to-coast possession in austral Africa in 1890, the only potential of the Empire lay in the large (but incompletely developed) colonies of Angola and Mozambique. These in Portuguese minds held the promise of a renewed prosperity and greatness. Further, with the heritage of having been Portuguese for so long, their ownership was to be defended at all costs. For this small European nation, the importance of the colonies was captured in an editorial by Dr Marcello Caetano in *O Mundo Português* (*Portuguese World*) that appeared in 1935: 'Africa is for us a moral justification and a *raison d'être* as a power. Without it we would be a small nation; with it, we are a great country'.[1] The growth of revolutionary climate in the *ultramar* during the 1950s clashed with this philosophy and the country's refusal to break the colonial bond and to decolonize. The 'winds of change' were blowing through Africa, but the Salazar regime refused to consider holding democratic elections or decolonizing.

Political opposition to Salazar and his policies was tolerated neither at home nor in the *ultramar*. An explosion was inevitable, and when it happened in 1961, the events in Angola and the seizing of Goa by India pushed Salazar to solidify the Portuguese commitment to defend the colonies. So strong was this feeling that it defied any voice of reason and foreclosed any retreat or compromise over African affairs. The Portuguese armed forces and treasure were thus pledged in full to preserve its Empire and the potential of renewed prosperity through an expensive counterinsurgency campaign.

Naval War Planning

The naval component in counterinsurgency often suffers from the primacy of the army and a lack of understanding on the part of

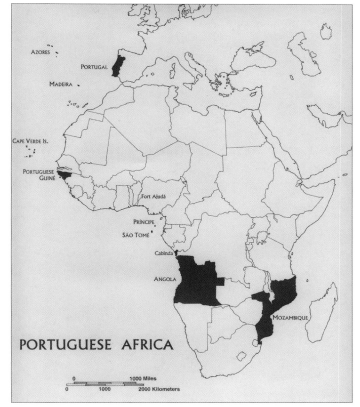

Portuguese Africa

national leaders as to how a riverine force can most effectively be used to support a land campaign. This primacy is understandable due to the fact that this form of war requires large numbers of light infantry to police the contested territory. All key infrastructure, villages and their inhabitants must be protected against an enemy who chooses when and where he will attack. Yet he must travel to the vulnerable installations and population centers to publish his message, recruit membership and raise money. To do this he must cross or use rivers, and in Africa, he must cross or use many of them. During the rainy season, these present formidable barriers. If they are policed, they may present very difficult or even impenetrable ones. In Lusophone Africa, where the fuzileiros distinguished themselves during the African campaigns, naval operations were most effective when they complemented the land campaign. In Angola, where there was excellent naval-land coordination, success was clearly achieved and the nationalist movements were completely stalemated. In Guiné and Mozambique, the two theaters where variations of a naval-land disconnect occurred, the enemy pressure proved difficult to contain.

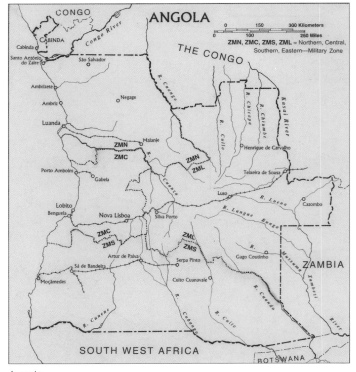

Angola.

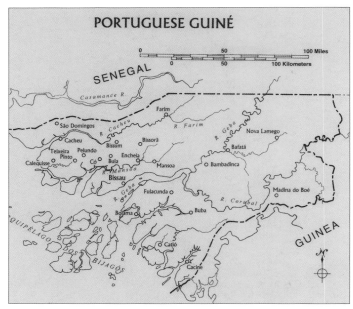

Guiné.

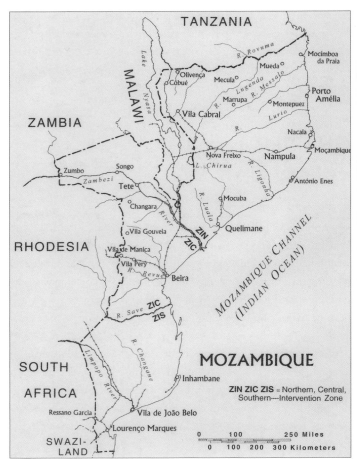

Mozambique.

The fuzileiros represented the naval-land bridge, and it fell to them to police the riverbanks and their approaches. Their amphibious capability was developed from scratch and reflected the depth and thoughtfulness of Portuguese Navy-thinking in building and deploying a substantial riverine capability in the hostile remoteness of a distant continent. To this day, Portuguese riverine strategy and its execution remain a successful and relevant model.

The leader in Portuguese naval thinking at the time was Captain Armando Júlio de Roboredo e Silva, and in February 1959, he initiated a request for an officer and three ratings to undergo Royal Marine training in what would become a first step in the reactivation of the fuzileiros.[2] As awareness of the coming conflict in Africa spread, a naval strategy for counterinsurgency there began to emerge. At the beginning of the war, Roboredo was promoted to Deputy Chief of

Staff, and then between 1963 and 1970 he served as Chief of Staff. Under his hand, naval policy crystallized into a firm operational plan with the means to execute it.

Roboredo, in developing his naval strategy, acknowledged that in a subversive war the navy extends its traditional twin tasks of securing the waterways for friendly use and of denying them to the enemy. Travel and traffic by water have always been cheaper and easier than by land, and thus in the rural, less developed areas (particularly in Africa), the contiguous waterways of a territory serve as vital arteries for commerce and war. These water bodies in particular hold great significance for military operations, as they present a natural obstacle to maneuver and provide ideal defensive terrain. They serve as natural boundaries to a battlefield; they are navigation aids and provide orientation; they are avenues of approach for combat and lines of communication for logistic operations. The enemy will likewise recognize their significance and value and seek to control the population, commerce and combat along these waterways. In any insurgency the population is the actual battleground, and the contest is for the loyalty of the people – thus a navy in counterinsurgency must fight for the effect that it can secure ashore where people live. Because of this land orientation, its operations will almost always be a joint enterprise with ground and air elements.

In addressing security in the Portuguese African territories, the navy was quick to recognize the obvious needs and consequently began to review its 'gunboat policy' of the previous century that had served it so well in the pacification of the *ultramar*.[3] This outdated policy, however, was hardly adequate in light of the situation developing in Africa –

Admiral Armando Júlio de Roboredo e Silva, Chief of Staff and founder of the modern fuzileiros, commissioning the first Naval Reserve medical doctor in 1968.
(Source: Estado-Maior da Armada and *Revista da Armada*)

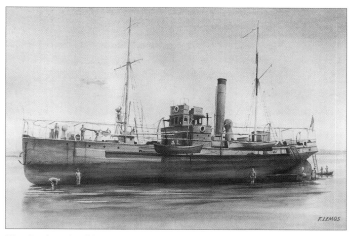

The Canhoneira *Limpopo*: one of the important vessels in Portuguese 'gunboat policy' that protected the littorals of Angola and Mozambique at the turn of the 20th century.
(Source: Estado-Maior da Armada and *Revista da Armada*)

so in January 1957, a new program was proposed: one that would be for Portugal as revolutionary as the shift from wooden to steel ships. It envisioned a small, tailored force that would be established in the *ultramar* as the basis for future expansion to address the new security situation and that would avoid infringing on the NATO obligations.[4] The composition of this force remained under some debate, and eventually it was settled as a force of fuzileiros and attendant inshore ships adapted to the African environment.[5] The assembly of this African Navy and its evolution became the most noteworthy naval development during the early years of the war.

The Portuguese requirements in Africa were embodied in three types of vessels: patrol boats (*lanchas de fiscalização*, or simply, LF) and landing craft (*lanchas de desembarque*, or simply, LD), both of various class sizes, and rubber boats (*botes de borracha*). All of these were a blend of the French and British experiences adapted to the conditions in Portuguese Africa. The LFs would be direct successors of the earlier coastal and river gunboats (*canhoneiras* and *lanchas-canhoneiras*, respectively) that had ranged from 38 tons to 492 tons displacement. Their mission would be one of patrolling Portuguese territorial waters, inspecting vessels suspected of supporting the insurgent movements and transporting small units of fuzileiros to be inserted ashore in rubber boats. Once ashore, the fuzileiros would gather intelligence, kill insurgents, disrupt food gathering and courier traffic, and make contact with the population. Because of the low-intensity nature of the conflict, it was not anticipated that these boats would face a conventional

land force with its relatively heavy crew-served weapons, as the French had experienced in Indochina. Instead they would encounter small bands of insurgents armed with what each could carry. These would include recoilless rifles, machine guns, rocket-propelled grenades (RPGs), mortars and mines – all dangerous enough in their own right, but seemingly not requiring the heavy armor or extensive armament of their forbearers. With these constraints removed, the navy was free to abandon the wood and steel shipbuilding materials of earlier years and explore modern, lightweight fiberglass and plywood hulls for the new LF concept. In this era, most boat-builders subscribed to the idea that 'fiberglass was for bathtubs and not boats'.[6] While a fiberglass boat was not novel at the time, such craft over six meters in length were rare. This did not inhibit the navy, however, from proceeding. The boats were designed for range, ease of maintenance, shallow draft, maneuverability and the capacity to carry small detachments of fuzileiros and their equipment for insertion ashore.

The same can be said for armament. It was thought that heavy cannon and automatic weapons were not needed and merely complicated boat design, as they and their ammunition stores raised the center of gravity. Simpler, lighter and highly potent weapons were available and had been proven in Indochina. The new, lighter hulls and selectively installed armor would simplify maintenance, lessen draft and add range, maneuverability and increased speed to the new boats. Fiberglass is easily repaired, and such a hull offered a backhanded sort of protection in that the insurgents' main heavy ordnance was the RPG that would go clean through fiberglass without detonating its armor-piercing warhead. The hole that it left was easy to repair. Armor would likewise raise the center of gravity and complicate design. It was always a question of judgment about how many of the numerous vulnerabilities should be protected and to what degree. Engines, fuel tanks, steering gear and large-caliber ammunition stores were always a priority. Further, the simplicity of design and reliability of well-tested and efficient diesel engines enabled long-range patrols in remote waters under harsh climatic conditions to be conducted with confidence.

With these notions in mind, the Portuguese Navy began to identify those boatyards capable of executing its concept on a trial

Bellatrix class patrol boat *Fomalhaut* (P 367) at speed on the Zaire River with its rubber boats alongside.
(Source: Personal archive of José Augusto Pires de Lima)

LFPs *Rigel* (P 378), *Altair* (P 377) and *Régulus* (P 369) in Angola at their acceptance ceremony on 21 February 1962 at the Luanda naval base. (Source: Estado-Maior da Armada and *Revista da Armada*)

LFG *Orion* (P 362) pierside at Ganturé on the River Cacheu, November 1972. (Source: Personal archive of Abel Melo e Sousa)

basis, as it had not developed its own competence of working in fiberglass. It ultimately chose a British yard to produce a small series of prototypes that combined simplicity with its experience in Africa and ordered its first three in a class of four 18-ton, small patrol boats (*lanchas de fiscalização pequenas*, or LFP). The *Antares* (P 360) was the first and class name, and the initial three craft were built in the United Kingdom in 1959. Each had an innovative moulded fiberglass hull 17 meters in length and was powered by two proven and reliable 250 horsepower Cummins-geared diesel engines driving conventional screw propellers. With a top speed of 18 knots, *Antares* had a range of 600 miles at full power. The speed was also satisfactory on overcoming the maximum current of eight to nine knots in the Zaire River and in putting the entire Congo Riverine Frontier of 80 miles within an eight-hour patrol. It carried no armor, and armament remained relatively light with a single bow-mounted 20 mm Oerlikon automatic cannon. It was equipped with short-range surface search radar to aid navigation along the twisting waterways at night and to detect enemy craft. Crew accommodation was spartan in keeping with budget and weight limitations. It and its sister ships *Sirius* (P 361) and *Vega* (P 362) were initially deployed to Goa. *Antares* escaped to Mozambique during the fall of Portuguese India in 1961, but the other two were lost. The last of the class, *Régulus* (P 369), was completed in Portugal in January 1962 on a hull imported from the United Kingdom and initially assigned duties on the Zaire River in Angola. Later it was transferred to Lake Niassa, where it undertook important and delicate missions.

The success of fiberglass as a hull material, coupled with the reliable diesel powerplant, encouraged the pursuit of another more capable class of LFPs. Accordingly, an additional eight vessels of the new and more robust 27.6-ton *Bellatrix* (P 363) class were ordered from *Bayerische Schiffbaugesellschaft GmbH* at Erlenbach am Main, West Germany and delivered between 1961 and 1962.[7] This class would continue with the Cummins engine specifically modified for the harsh tropical environment. The first three of the '30-tonners', as they were nicknamed, were assigned to Patrol Squadron Guiné and the next five to Patrol Squadron Zaire. The *Bellatrix* design was likewise very successful, with its augmented capabilities and improvements gained from experience with the *Antares*, and this positive development

increased confidence to pursue further construction at home. In 1968, the remaining five vessels of the class were built in the Alfeite shipyard. From these the first three were deployed to Guiné and the remaining two to Porto Amélia, Mozambique. Those deployed to Guiné were fitted additionally with 37 mm rocket launchers.

The large patrol boats (*lanchas de fiscalização grandes*, or LFG) played a prominent role in all of the theaters, but particularly in Guiné, where they were the most significant naval units. The initial series was the 210-ton *Arcos* class, and these were followed by the 310-ton *Cacine* class.[8] These were steel-hulled and armed with two Bofors 40 mm cannon and two MG 42 7.62 mm machine guns, and were often equipped with multiple launchers each loaded with thirty-two 37 mm rockets. The LFGs brought more robust firepower and other capabilities to the fight along the rivers, as well as a seagoing capability. Because of their size, they were less stealthy than the smaller launches and less able to operate in shallow water. Nevertheless, they were the queens of the rivers. Both the LFP and LFG vessels undertook patrol and surveillance missions, performed escort duties for landing craft and acted in a limited role as transports. There were other deployments and visits to the theaters by larger warships, particularly to Guiné, but they were occasional and less meaningful.

In addition to the need for patrol boats, there was a very practical need for landing craft of three sizes: small, medium and large. These

LDP 108 disembarking fuzileiros into their rubber boats on the Zaire River. (Source: Estado-Maior da Armada and *Revista da Armada*)

LDG 102 discharging vehicles at low tide; August 1974, Guiné. (Source: Photograph by Alexandre da Fonseca – courtesy of *Revista da Armada*)

A Bofors 40 mm autocannon, with Stiffkey sights mounted on the forward deck of an LFG, and manned by fuzileiros. (Source: Personal archive of Luís Sanches de Baêna)

moved not only troops in the traditional way of amphibious warfare, but also military cargo, and maintained lines of communication with the population in areas that relied on rivers over a primitive road system. Unfortunately, the United Kingdom and the United States – the two countries that had done the most development work on landing craft – were advocates of decolonization and reluctant to sell these craft directly to Portugal to pursue a 'colonial' war in Africa. Using an indirect process partially to solve the problem, Portugal employed a private commercial firm to contract with a similar US firm in the early 1960s for the purchase of a number of old surplus World War Two-era landing craft medium, or LCMs.[9] The craft acquired had all experienced a hard life, and many were in poor condition. They were shipped to Lisbon, where they were renovated (and in some cases, practically rebuilt) in the shipyard at Santos. When delivered to the navy in 1963, they were designated *lanchas de desembarque médias* (LDM). It is difficult to know today just how many of the US LCM-type craft were acquired through this process, but it is probably safe to say that about one-third of the total number of LDMs were US in origin.[10] *Comandante* Beradino Cadete, one of the two officers in charge of the LD project, remembers the initial purchase of 25 landing craft from the United States being in two lots of 15 and 10 respectively.[11] He also noted that, despite their sad state of repair, their Gray Marine engines were quite serviceable, as they had been rebuilt in the United States

through a contract with Fairbanks Morse prior to delivery.[12] There must have been some considerable attrition from the initial buy, as by December 1969, records indicate that 18 US-built and 17 locally-built LDMs were in operation.[13]

The small and large landing craft – called *lanchas de desembarque pequenas* (LDP) and *grandes* (LDG) respectively – were adapted from a British concept, just as the LDM had been adapted from an American one. The plans for these craft originally came from the British Admiralty in 1962 and were modified from those of the World War Two-era landing craft assault (LCA) and landing craft tank (LCT) designs.[14] The modifications made in Lisbon were intended to keep the craft versatile, yet simple and thus inexpensive. These vessels were built in Portugal in the Mondego shipyards over the intervening decade, and the last was delivered in August 1973.[15] The LDG series had two classes: the *Alfange* class at 480 tons and the *Bombarda* class at 652 tons.[16] In the case of the LDG, there was one important change in the design of the ramp: it was originally intended to disembark heavy armored vehicles, and as a consequence of the change in requirements for African operations, was lightened to accommodate only personnel and light vehicles.[17] Armored vehicles were of little use in a counterinsurgency and particularly in the terrain of Portuguese Africa.

The operation of these LD vessels was different from that of other traditional ones in that, with their flat bottoms, shallow drafts and anaemic powerplants, they were difficult to maneuver and demanded skilled seamanship and extensive experience.[18] The missions of the LDs were extraordinarily important during the war not only for specific military operations, but also in cooperation with the civil authorities in moving people, local market goods and other assorted cargo. These were often conducted under the particularly difficult climatic and hydrographic conditions of severely restricted channels, narrow rivers, strong currents, heavy seas and monsoon weather.[19] The LDs were manned by petty officers and ratings who bore great responsibility in their operation and endured long assignments under spartan conditions. Accommodation was bare, and ventilation and air conditioning on the vessels non-existent. The crew was exposed to the brutal tropical sun above deck and to a furnace-like atmosphere below, where privacy became a casualty of combat. The performance of the LD crews under some of the most difficult operating conditions imaginable remains one

NRP *Pacheco Pereira* (F 337) disembarking fuzileiros in the north of Angola during late 1961.
(Source: Estado-Maior da Armada and *Revista da Armada*)

LFG *Orion* (P 362) pierside at Ganturé on the River Cacheu, November 1972, with two LDMs alongside in a nested mooring.
(Source: Personal archive of Abel Melo e Sousa)

of the unsung naval contributions not only to military successes with the fuzileiros, but also to humanitarian support. By the end of the conflict in 1974, a total of 89 vessels had been either built in Portugal or acquired from the United States: 26 LDPs, six LDGs and 57 LDMs.[20] Seventy-three of them were employed in Africa: 51 in Guiné, 15 in Angola and seven in Mozambique.

The third leg of the African Navy was the rubber boat, which could be launched from the *João Coutinho* class corvette or any of the LFs or LDs and facilitate fuzileiro pursuit of insurgent elements along the riverbanks and littorals. The inflatable rubber boat, which was the 1934 brainchild of Pierre Debroutelle (an engineer with the French firm of Zodiac), remained in its design shops until after World War Two, when military interest underwrote its more mature development. In 1952, Alain Bombard made an Atlantic Ocean crossing in a Zodiac Mark III from Las Palmas in the Canary Islands to Barbados and thereby established its true viability. Acquired in great numbers by the navy from Zodiac, this small three-meter-long raft could be easily carried on an LF or LD or larger vessel and launched with its crew to execute varied tasks. It was powered by either an outboard engine or paddles.[21] It was a sturdy and reliable craft, with its multiple air compartments, and served the navy well.

The uses of the boat, ultimately named the *Zebro III*, were many and varied. It was somewhat the Jeep or helicopter of the waterways in that it served a host of missions from patrols to ambushes; to hydrographic work; to alongside maintenance; and to anything in between. Its uses were limited only by one's imagination. It proved extremely useful in patrolling the restricted canals and other shallow bodies of a river for which there was no other means of access. Its stability and ruggedness were nowhere more evident than on the Zaire River, where tree trunks and other dangerous debris were commonplace threats to a rupture in its air compartments, and where the large wakes of merchantmen threatened to capsize it. Daily maintenance of the boats and engines was critical despite their simplicity and rugged construction. Most important to our story, however, was its use by the fuzileiros in securing the river systems of the *ultramar*.

Operations

The primary mission of the navy in subversive war or insurgency was to prevent the enemy from using the navigable waterways for any of its purposes. This generally involved conducting coastal and littoral patrols to prevent insurgent use of the sea approaches to support subversive activities inland, and likewise conducting the more complicated river patrols to prevent their varied enemy use. In the coastal and littoral areas, the sort of gruelling and monotonous routine of identifying and inspecting small boat traffic was mind-numbing. The search for scarce targets and the repetition of negative results severely tested crews. If vigilance slackened, however, the enemy would be quick to notice.

Riverine operations were very restive and posed problems with their channelization that limited military flexibility. They thus carried a higher risk than did ground operations. Both defensive and offensive operations were required to control the river: defensively, positions were occupied and security measures taken at key points along the waterway, particularly at crossings and constrictions; offensively, sector patrols were conducted continuously somewhere along the river, as active patrolling kept the enemy reactive, while government forces were proactive.

There were two general actions that were used to dissuade enemy activity and force a modification in his behavior: the first was simply the establishment of a presence on the rivers, their meanders, braided channels, canals and oxbow lakes; the second was adding an element of surprise to this presence. Establishing presence was the most expensive of the two, as to be effective it required a large number of men – either on land along the riverbank, or under way in boats – to provide a high revisit time and thereby the impression of a constant presence of government forces. Because it was impossible for troops to be everywhere, there were inevitable lapses in this presence through which the enemy could move. He watched the movement of forces and noted their pattern of behavior. From his analysis of these activities he was able to discern the holes in coverage and move to exploit these gaps. The alternative to tying down many numbers of troops in this sort of coverage was to introduce surprise. The routine then had an unpredictable aspect, and the enemy was thrown off-balance. With this uncertainty, the insurgent was forced to change his behavior. He was dissuaded from using the now more dangerous river and forced to use other, more lengthy detours or hopefully to abandon his project altogether.

On the rivers of the *ultramar*, one of the key tools of surprise was the imaginative use of the rubber boat. It represented a great economy of means in its flexibility and ability to carry a small force of fuzileiros

Zebro III boats operating in 'silent mode' in the Bulicoco Island canals of the Zaire River.
(Source: Estado-Maior da Armada and *Revista da Armada*)

for clandestine insertion ashore to conduct an ambush or simply to perform a reconnaissance patrol. Rubber boats generally operated minimally in pairs for mutual support and carried three to four fuzileiros each. They would sortie either from a fixed base on the riverbank or lakeside, or from the moving base of a ship or patrol craft. The latter was less expensive and less vulnerable than a land base and offered the further advantage of operational flexibility. This flexibility translated into a varied and irregular pattern of patrols as to the time of day and to the mode of operation.

One of the most common methods of conducting any rubber boat operation was to tow them alongside an LF. This particular configuration allowed the fuzileiros to board the boats and detach quickly either from an LF at speed, or one slowing to investigate an unidentified contact. This posture also permitted substantial flexibility in operations. For instance, often at night an LF would pass along the targeted area of a river and launch its two boats with their fuzileiros without slowing. The boats would then maneuver by silently drifting with the current and waiting for the enemy to expose himself, or by silently paddling to an appropriate site to set an ambush. This was particularly difficult, for the fuzileiros – paddling quietly into the utter darkness of the river margins – could use no light and make no sound for fear of losing surprise and alerting the enemy. The riverbank at night, with the inky blackness of its vegetal cover, was a tricky operating environment.

Raids, reconnaissance patrols, or ambushes could likewise be set by inserting fuzileiros ashore via rubber boat. This maneuver was generally performed at night, for it allowed the force to move in silence under cover of darkness from the water, overland, to spring its assault in the early-morning hours before dawn when the enemy slept his soundest and fuzileiro presence was least expected. In approaching a target, fuzileiros traveled cross-country and avoided roads because of mines, particularly in Guiné. The normal range of such a patrol was limited to about 30 kilometers due to the difficult terrain and particularly to the tidal action in Guiné, and could last as long as two days. Following the operation, the fuzileiros would return to their point of embarkation and subsequently be recovered by rubber boats from an LF or LD. The aim of these operations was to keep the enemy off-balance and never to permit him any feeling of security.

If an LF were stopping to investigate a suspicious contact at night, it would launch its boats and direct them through the darkness by radio

along compass bearings based on the radar return. This procedure was normally used only for short distances of less than four miles. Usually the fuzileiros would carry a radar reflector in the boat to aid in course corrections to the target; however, if this were lost, then a steel helmet would be raised on a pole as a makeshift alternative.[22]

Boats would also be launched in daylight prior to reaching a target area and follow the LF after an appropriate interval. This tactic was pursued in the hope that the enemy would believe the area safe following the passage of the LF, expose himself in conducting his activity and be caught by the second patrol of boats. Many times, patrols of fuzileiros would be only partially recovered from a target area as a decoy, leaving a force hidden in ambush. The variation in tactics was limited only to the imagination, but the rubber boat was invariably an integral and important part in adding flexibility to African naval operations and proved itself well in the conflict.

As the conflict progressed, the navy expanded in an amphibious direction to address the African littoral and riverine environment. Its coastal and riverine fleet in Africa grew from 15 patrol ships, 10 patrol boats and a gunboat in 1960 to 17 patrol ships, 43 patrol boats and no less than 83 landing craft of various types and sizes in 1970 – an expansion from 26 to 143 units without any rigid plan.[23] The vessels ranged from small patrol craft of 30 tons to considerably more capable craft of 200 tons.[24] Its amphibious force of landing craft in three different sizes of increasing capability was literally created from scratch.[25] This loosely-guided development rather followed the demonstrated needs of each theater commander. Unfortunately, there were continuing requests from each for additional ships that resulted in an almost inexorable expansion across Africa. This constant augmentation caused the Minister of the Navy in September 1970 to declare that there would be no more ships without a 'full justification'. The African Navy consequently stabilized, and at the end of 1973 it stood at 137 units, with which it had to provide security over approximately 920 miles of navigable rivers and 120 miles of the Lake Niassa Coast.[26] While it also had to provide coastal security, this was not a substantial factor in either Angola (Atlantic Ocean) or Mozambique (Indian Ocean) because of the lack of insurgent seaborne capability and the distance of any fighting from these coasts. This was a positive development, as planners had anticipated an insurgent effort similar to that encountered by the French Navy in Algeria and Indochina, and the US Navy in Vietnam, in which the insurgents attempted to supply their forces by sea disguised as merchants or fishermen. This attempted logistical link necessitated a rigorous and costly coastal inspection effort by the French, South Vietnamese and US Navies.

The fleet expansion also included an augmentation and shift in types of personnel. In 1946, there were 719 officers and 5,550 men.[27] By 1960, there were 887 officers and 8,583 men – a 50 percent expansion.[28] By 1974, total personnel had more than doubled to 19,500 officers and men – of whom 3,400 were fuzileiros.[29] The fuzileiros had their origin in the formation of the *Terço da Armada Real* (Royal Naval Regiment) by the Portuguese Crown in 1618. Deactivated in 1890, they remained so until 1961 except for a brief period from 1924 to 1926. Responsible for maritime and riverine security, the fuzileiros played key and varying roles in all of the African theaters – of which we will hear more shortly.

Holden Roberto, head of the UPA/FNLA.
(Source: Personal archive of Abel Melo e Sousa)

Mobutu, President of Zaire.

Agostinho Neto, head of the
MPLA.

The Enemy

In the 1960s, Portugal faced opponents across three fronts with an aggregate of 27,000 troops. The UPA (*Uniao das Populações de Angola*, or Union of Angolan Peoples), headed by Holden Roberto, was based in the former Belgian Congo and supported by its President, Joseph-Desiré Mobutu. It threatened Angola with an active force of about 6,200 men. In March 1962, the UPA reorganized itself to include additional small nationalist groups; to rename itself the FNLA (*Frente Nacional de Libertação de Angola*, or National Front for the Liberation of Angola); and to establish a government in exile named GRAE (*Governo da República de Angola no Exílio*, or Government of the Republic of Angola in Exile). Little of substance was accomplished. A frustrated Jonas Savimbi, Roberto's 'Foreign Minister', formally broke with the UPA/FNLA in July 1964 and eventually formed the third nationalist movement in Angola: UNITA (*União Nacional para a Independência Total de Angola*, or the National Union for the Total Independence of Angola). UNITA, operating from an area within South-East Angola under terms that were negotiated with the Portuguese, mustered about 500 men who were restricted to fighting the MPLA. The MPLA (*Movimento Popular de Libertação de Angola*, or Popular Movement for the Liberation of Angola), headed by Agostinho Neto, also contested Angola from the Congo but was not a significant military threat until 1966, when it opened its Eastern Front from Zambia with an estimated strength of 4,700.[30] The PAIGC (*Partido Africano da Independência da Guiné e Cabo Verde*, or African Party for the Independence of Guiné and Cape Verde), headed by Amílcar Cabral, first threatened Guiné with a small force in 1962 from its sanctuaries in Guinée-Conakry and Senegal – and by 1973, had 5,000 regular troops and 1,500 militia. By the early 1970s, FRELIMO (*Frente de Libertação de Moçambique*, or Front for the

Liberation of Mozambique), originally headed by Eduado Mondlane, had an active force of 7,200 regulars and 2,400 popular militia across the northern border of Mozambique in the sanctuary of Tanzania.[31] The various insurgent units were spread across three distinct theaters of operations and carried various degrees of competence.

In Angola, following the 15 March 1961 attacks in the north, the UPA and MPLA forces immediately across the northern border represented more of a policing problem than any threat of a major assault because of internal political friction, poor training, indiscipline and logistic weakness. Later in the east, however, the MPLA became a difficult and skilled opponent operating from the newly-available Zambian sanctuary. In Guiné, the PAIGC were always a highly motivated and formidable foe and were aided by the terrain and neighboring sanctuaries that helped to reduce the colony to a besieged enclave. In Mozambique, FRELIMO was isolated in the north of the theater and faced long distances over often open and sparsely-populated terrain to engage concentrations of the population, or Portuguese troop formations. With some exceptions, the insurgents in all theaters operated in small bands and traveled long distances to set ambushes, collect taxes, gather food and recruit troops. Rarely did they stay and fight. As they either used the rivers for travel or corridors of penetration, the military job of the Portuguese Navy and its fuzileiros was to control the waterways in enemy areas, inhibit insurgent movement, counter these small groups through ambushes in the riverine areas, project power ashore and supply villages and troops. Alongside these duties were the political ones of reassuring the population with recurring naval presence, and psychosocial support and gathering intelligence. As we shall see, the fuzileiros did this well.

Fuzileiros

In designing the force structure for the African Navy, Roboredo envisioned a series of ship classes to patrol the coastline and rivers of the *ultramar*. On each of these vessels there would be a detachment of fuzileiros, for a key part of controlling the littorals of these waterways was the control of the coasts and riverbanks. This meant that the navy must have a force prepared to project power ashore from its vessels. Roboredo thus saw an immediate and potential need for a small nucleus of specialized, elite troops who were trained to operate in the littoral

Jonas Savimbi, head of UNITA.

Amílcar Cabral, head of the PAIGC.

Eduardo Mondlane, head of FRELIMO.

There were, from the earliest times of the Portuguese Navy, small forces of army troops on board the King's ships to fulfil a need for light infantry. It was not, however, until 1585 that specialization within the navy occurred with the introduction of specific instruction in the use of artillery and firearms for certain elements in the crews of ships bound for India. This instruction was aimed at providing a more robust protection for the ships themselves, as well as the ports in this theater. More formally the *Corpo de Fuzileiros* can trace its origin to the creation of the *Terço da Armada da Coroa de Portugal* (Naval Regiment of the Portuguese Crown), which was formed in April of 1621 to supply naval troops for embarkation on these ships. It had the distinction of being the first permanently-organized military unit in Portugal. This position had given it the singular privilege of always being to the right in any military ceremony and of breaking ranks ahead of all others in formation. The embarked infantrymen performed duties as sailors, as artillerymen, as boarding and landing parties, and as defenders against hostile boarding parties depending on the requirements at hand. They distinguished themselves particularly in helping to reduce the pirate menace along the Portuguese trade routes.[33] These troops served aboard all vessels following the coast of Africa, across the Indian Ocean as far to the east as Japan, and across the Atlantic to South America. They became the personal guard of the Kings of Portugal and were integrated into the expeditionary forces in pacifying the African territories. They manned the numerous *fortalezas* (fortresses) that protected the trading enclaves along the coasts of Portuguese exploration. Over the years, the force underwent many diverse designations, such as: *Infantaria da Marinha* (Naval Infantry), *Brigada Real de Marinha* (Royal Naval Brigade), *Regimento da Armada* (Naval Regiment), *Batalhão Naval* (Naval Battalion), *Corpo de Marinheiros Militares* (Corps of Naval Soldiers) and *Brigada da Guarda Naval* (Brigade of Naval Guards).

The term 'fuzileiro', however, first appeared in the navy in 1797 with the formation of the *Brigada Real de Marinha* and its division into three groups according to the primary specialties of its members. The first was composed of 10 companies of *Artilheiros-Marinheiros* (Artillery Sailors), who were responsible for shipboard artillery and forts and gunpowder warehouses, as well as other tasks peculiar to artillery.[34] The second was composed of 12 companies of *Fuzileiros-Marinheiros* (Fusilier-Sailors), who were responsible for landing operations, shipboard defense against boarding parties and the security of the Naval Arsenal.[35] The third was composed of 10 companies of *Artífices e Lastradores-Marinheiros* (Artificers and Ballasters-Sailors), who plied their skills on board the King's ships and in his shipyards.[36] The full strength of the brigade was 5,222 men.

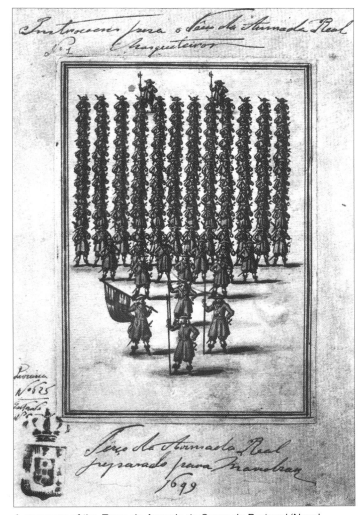

A company of the *Terço da Armada da Coroa de Portugal* (Naval Regiment of the Portuguese Crown).
(Source: Estado-Maior da Armada and *Revista da Armada*)

and whose numbers could be expanded rapidly in the event of any emergency.[32] This need would become increasingly apparent with the Portuguese expulsion from the anachronistic Fort São João Batista de Ajudá in Dahomey (present-day Benin), the assault on the cruise liner *Santa Maria* and developments in the north of Angola – all occurring throughout 1960 and into the early months of 1961. In 1959, he took the first steps to re-establish the *Corpo de Fuzileiros*, or Marine Corps.

A contingent of fuzileiros accompanied King John IV and the Portuguese Court when, because of the French invasion of the Iberian Peninsula, it fled to Brazil in November 1807. Later in 1822 when John's eldest son, Pedro IV, declared himself Emperor Pedro I of the Kingdom of Brazil and broke with Portugal, this contingent formed the basis for the Brazilian *Fuzileiros Navais* (or Naval Fuzileiros) of today.[37]

The brigade was reorganized in 1807 and again in 1808 – resulting in a reduction in its overall strength to 2,992 men. Again in 1823, the brigade was reduced to two battalions of eight companies each, or a total strength of 1,647 men. In October 1836, the brigade was reformed as the *Regimento da Armada* with four battalions of four companies each, or a total strength of 1,815 men.[38] In January 1837, the *Batalhão Naval* was created in yet another reorganization and consisted of eight companies for an overall strength of 681 men; the battalion structure mirrored that of the regiment with minor exceptions.[39] In 1840, the battalion was augmented to 1,200 men. By 1851, the battalion held only 835 men and was replaced with the *Corpo de Marinheiros Militares* with a strength of 22 companies. Historically the fuzileiros had been light infantry, but with this change came a heavier, more robust force. Its troops were instructed in seamanship, infantry tactics, small arms skills and landing party operations. Each embarked company had a squad of artillerymen-cabin boys who were practiced in gunnery, gunlaying and shipboard working parties. In 1875, the corps was reorganized into three divisions: each with a section of fuzileiros and artillerymen. These troops assumed the duties of sailors and general-purpose troops. Another reorganization in 1884 created in the corps six companies of fuzileiros, as well as companies of lookouts, artillerymen, firemen and stokers, and storekeepers. With so many reorganizations over a relatively short period, one might wonder if it were a force in search of a clearly-defined mission. The corps was consequently dissolved in 1890 under King Carlos I, and its duties assigned to other entities. It was briefly reactivated between 1924 and 1926 as the *Brigada da Guarda Naval* to furnish security for naval bases and ships, a forerunner of the *Companhas de Fuzileiros* (Companies of Fuzileiros), but again it was dissolved.

The need for another reactivation became evident well before the 1960 developments in the Belgian Congo. Roboredo anticipated that the coming conflict in Africa would be a protracted one and moved

to make the necessary preparations. The notion of a shipborne force able to project power ashore met with stiff resistance from numerous quarters. The arguments against the development of such a capability lay in the view that the navy was unprepared for a land war; that in the coming war, there would be no need for amphibious forces; and that the building of this type of force would further dilute the already-meager navy budget. Roboredo did not accept these arguments and dispatched staff to the army center for Special Forces at Lamego, to Spain, to Algeria and to the United Kingdom to examine the varied approaches in establishing such a proposed force.[40] While this research initially favored the British model of a Royal Marine force structure with its Special Boat Service and use of rubber boats, the French model – with its refinements through the Indochina experience – held valuable lessons and would be used increasingly as the program matured.

Things were accelerated by an anticipation of developments in Angola and particularly by a plea from the Naval Command there on 11 April 1960 that voiced concern about the general security situation in the *ultramar* and in Angola in particular.[41] The naval commander in Angola recommended that a specialized landing force be established to operate from patrol boats and that it be instructed in infantry tactics and procedures. He also sought immediate permission to form a company of naval infantry within his own command and to train it. In response, Roboredo – now a *comodoro*, or commodore – sought approval from the Chief of Staff of the Navy not only for the force in Angola, but also for the formal establishment of a larger, permanent force for wider employment throughout the *ultramar*. He also suggested that foreign training be sought initially to establish a small cadre of officers and petty officers to serve as instructors in a school for training naval infantry.

Indeed, Roboredo had at first appealed to the French in early 1959 for a proposal to train a small contingent of Portuguese officers and petty officers at the École *des Fusiliers* at the Centre Siroco at Cap Matifou near Alger. This small group, upon completion of training, would help set the course for its own service by supplying the future instructors in Portugal. The French were happy to oblige; however, the difficulty with their program was that basic officer-training ran eight months, with an additional two for specialized 'commando' instruction. For enlisted personnel the periods were five and three months respectively.[42] The British responded with a more focused

The Portuguese Court lands in Brazil, 7 March 1808, with a contingent of fuzileiros; from the painting by Miranda Júnior.

The first four fuzileiros after completing their Royal Marine instruction. From left: Ludgero Silva, Mário Claudino, Second Lieutenant Pascoal Rodrigues and João Santinhos – all wearing their Royal Marine berets. (Source: Escola de Fuzileiros)

course of nine weeks in purely commando training in contrast to the French, who had insisted on basic training prior to their commando course.[43] Although the French training had been Roboredo's first choice, it was far too lengthy in comparison to the British proposal, and the decision was subsequently made to use the more specialized and shorter Royal Marine instruction.[44] Accordingly, three lieutenants (*segundo tenentes*) and three petty officers were designated to attend the Royal Marine commando course in Lympstone, South Devon.[45] Second Lieutenant Alberto Manuel Barreto Pascoal Rodrigues and three petty officers – Ludjero dos Santos Silva, João Cândido dos Santos Santinhos and Mário José Baptista Claudino – actually completed the course on 30 September 1960 and returned to Lisbon shortly thereafter.

In February 1961, the first formal organizational steps were taken with the creation of a training program for prospective fuzileiro sergeants and soldiers to prepare them for deployment in the *ultramar*.[46] Sergeants would later be recruited from fuzileiro corporals who would be promoted on successful completion of the sergeant course. The initial course enrolled between 35 and 40 men recruited from within the navy and was designed to provide the training of troops capable of amphibious landings, of safeguarding naval installations and of acting as a security force in coastal regions. It was conducted as part of the *Corpo de Marinheiros*, which was a dependency of Group No. 2 of the naval schools in Alfeite. The training ground itself occupied land just south across the Tagus River from Lisbon and was borrowed from the army. It was ideal in that it comprised the difficult thickets and forests of Alfeite and the Quinta do Antelmo, the swampy marshes immediately south of this area and the dramatic mountains of the nearby Serra da Arrábida. Three subsequent and challenging courses were held in these areas before the specialized and formal school for the fuzileiros was completed at nearby Vale de Zebro in June.[47] The value of having its own specialized school was that subsequent experience in the *ultramar* enabled the navy to modify the training to fit specific developments in each theater and the shifting methods of insurgent fighting. From this trained pool of graduates came the personnel to form the first detachment of special fuzileiros (*Destacamento de Fuzileiros Especiais No. 1,* or DFE 1) in October 1961, which deployed to Angola the following month.[48] This and subsequent deployments are detailed in the tables at the end of this chapter.

To form additional units of fuzileiros, the navy continued to recruit candidates from within its own ranks. Initially this process was seen as a 'conversion' program for sailors and was thus termed a 'conversion course'. Because recruitment from within was quickly exhausted, it became necessary to implement a broader effort targeted at the civil population as a second source. Over the course of the war, these two sources were able to fulfil the need of the School of Fuzileiros and its special fuzileiros course by appealing to the desire of the applicants to be part of an elite force of growing fame in Africa, although as we shall see, this was not an easy or straightforward task… Fuzileiro officers on the other hand were recruited from among the graduates of the regular course at the Naval Academy (*Escola Naval*) and, later, those from the Naval Engineers (*Engenheiros Maquinistas Navais*) and Naval Supply (*Administração Naval*) classes. These numbers were complemented by cadets undergoing the Naval Reserve Officer course at the same institution.

The training course conducted at the School of Fuzileiros comprised two phases: first, there was the basic recruit and technical training in military fundamentals, and the aspects unique to the fuzileiros. This phase was complemented by a second in which those graduates selected to be special fuzileiros (*fuzileiros especiais*, or FZE) were integrated into detachments of special fuzileiros (*destacamento de fuzileiros especiais*, or DFE), while the other candidates were designated naval fuzileiros (*fuzileiros navais*, or FZ) and assigned to companies of fuzileiros (*companhias de fuzileiros*, or CF).[49]

Comandante Guilherme Alpoim Calvão, the most decorated naval officer in Portuguese history, described his training to become a FZE in the late summer of 1963:

> I found the specialised course for FZEs physically very gruelling, a characteristic that compelled a close coexistence between officers, sergeants, and corporals and consequently cultivated a solid bonding among them. This was very typical of people of the sea in that sailors were always in the habit of living in confined spaces and were together and equally subjected to the same risks from the commander to the newest seaman. This process strongly defined fuzileiro units. The course required hard proof, such as a march of fifty kilometres in the Arrábida with the objective of the Pico de São Luiz, or another on the coast of Peniche with a finish at the School of Fuzileiros, where one must enter undetected or suffer the penalty of being interned in a "concentration camp" until all had completed the exercise. There were also obstacle courses filled with combat and mud. This training gave us an excellent physical preparation and above all a perfect understanding of arms.[50]

DFEs were considered elite units and in fact were the Special Forces of the navy. They were composed of men with special abilities, inordinate self-confidence and undaunted courage, and were proud to wear their distinguishing beret and badge. They were also, as a rule, imaginatively led and noted for their unit flexibility and mobility. These characteristics gave them a unique advantage in finding and engaging insurgents effectively in the most adverse operating conditions, and in exploiting the slimy tropical environment that was habitually found bordering the lakes and rivers of the *ultramar*.

The DFEs originally in 1962 comprised 75 men (two officers, seven sergeants, eight corporals, 14 able seamen and 44 seamen), and later in 1967, this manning level was raised to 80 men (four officers, six sergeants, 14 corporals, 32 able seamen and 24 seamen).[51] The organization was also modified in each theater to address the operating environment, and in fact, each detachment developed expertise in a particular geographic area and thus tended to be reassigned there to exploit this strength. Originally, a DFE consisted of four sections of infantry and one support section, and these sections were variously called assault (*grupos de assault*, or GA) or combat groups, depending

The obstacle course filled with mud, as described by *Comandante* Alpoim Calvão. (Source: Escola de Fuzileiros)

The DFE Training Centre for the African fuzileiros in Bolama that housed their barracks, classrooms, messing facilities, and a parade ground. (Source: Arquivo Central da Marinha)

Lieutenant Nuno Vieira Matias at his special fuzileiro graduation ceremony from the 19th *Fuzileiros Especiais* course (5 June–30 September 1967). He is receiving his FZE beret and designator badge – and many years later became the Chief of Staff of the Navy. (Source: Escola de Fuzileiros)

on the theater. By 1968, the number of officers was increased to four to permit the commanding officer to have an officer lead each of the assault groups. The DFE could also be organized into two assault groups, each with two sharp-shooter sections armed with bazookas, MG-42 machine guns, mortars, RPGs and logistical support as needed.[52] Indeed, to increase unit flexibility, sections were further divided into sub-groups or teams of four or five men in Angola and Mozambique, or a squad of three men in Guiné, each with a specific task of assault or support to add flexibility in exploiting the terrain and enemy deployment and in bringing surprise and overwhelming force on an unsuspecting foe. Subsequently there were DFEs, with three officers and 75 men, and even two officers and 70 men.[53]

Toward the end of the 1960s, the navy began to recruit its fuzileiro officers from within the fuzileiro community, and there appeared the first of a long line of officers who had risen from the ranks to command a number of the DFEs and CFs.[54] The fuzileiros in a DFE over the span of the war tended increasingly to be veterans who had elected to make the navy a career following either their initial six-year term of enlistment as a volunteer, or four-year term as a drafted recruit.[55] This trend translated into a high level of experience and

unit cohesiveness, as the veterans were skilled and motivated. These characteristics were particularly apparent when units experienced the stress of combat and were forced to perform effectively in the proverbial Clausewitzian 'fog of war'. During the war, each DFE was deployed to the *ultramar* for a period of about two years (normally 23 months, but a little less in Guiné), at the end of which it would return to continental Portugal (the *metrópole*) to refit and rest. Following a year-long period spent in replacing losses and undergoing refresher training, the unit would again deploy to the *ultramar*. The DFEs were designated from 1 to 13, and this number proved to be adequate to maintain the deployment cycle of 10 in the *ultramar* and three in the *metrópole*. Additionally, there were three African DFEs established in Guiné (DFE 21, 22 and 23) in the early 1970s and disbanded in August 1974. These were trained at the Centre for Preparation of African Fuzileiros (*Centro de Preparação de Fuzileiros Africans*) located at Boloma and led by officers and sergeants who had graduated from the School of Fuzileiros in the Vale de Zebro. The facility was established in February 1970 and deactivated in August 1974.

The CFs were composed of 120 men and were trained for and charged with the security and immediate defense of naval installations and the security of the waterways of the *ultramar*. Additionally, they conducted inspections of maritime and riverine traffic, reconnaissance patrols and ambushes in the contested zones of the rivers and lakes of the *ultramar*. Often they collaborated with army units in specific operations, or furnished support for moving army troops by water. The CFs held designations numbering from 1 to 11 during the war, although there was a 12th at the end of the war, and this number proved adequate for a proper deployment cycle that maintained nine CFs (two CFs in Guiné, four in Angola and three in Mozambique) in the *ultramar* and two in the *metrópole* on rest and refitting duties. These were on a similar rotation cycle as the DFEs.

The first DFE deployed to the *ultramar* on 10 November 1961 and the first CF on 31 May 1962 – both to Angola. This was the beginning of a force that expanded to over a thousand FZEs in DFEs and another thousand fuzileiros in CFs deployed across the *ultramar* – and in subsequent chapters, we will explore this development.

Table 1

Naval Disposition (units of fuzileiros), 1961–1974

DFE *(destacamentos de fuzileiros especiais)* and CF *(companhias de fuzileiros)*

Dates		Guiné		Angola		Mozambique		Total	
Year	Month	DFE	CF	DFE	CF	DFE	CF	DFE	CF
1961	November			1				1	
1962	May			1	1			1	1
	June	1		1	1			2	1
	August	1		2	1			3	1
	October	1		2	1		1	3	2
1963	February	1		3	1		1	4	2
	June	1	1	3	1		1	4	3
	September	1	1	4	1		1	5	3
	October	2	1	4	1		1	6	3
	November	3	1	4	1		1	7	3
1964	February	4	1	4	1		1	8	3
	November	4	1	4	2	1	1	9	4
1965	March	4	1	3	2	1	1	8	4
	June	4	1	3	2	2	1	9	4
	November	4	1	3	2	3	2	10	5
1966	August	4	2	3	3	3	2	9	7
	December	4	2	2	3	3	2	9	7
1967	February	4	2	2	3	4	2	10	7
1968	August	4	2	2	4	4	2	10	8
1969		4	2	2	4	4	2	10	8
1970	June	5	2	2	4	4	2	11	8
1971		5	2	2	4	4	2	11	8
1972		5	2	2	4	4	2	11	8
1973	April	5	2	2	4	3	3	10	9
1974	February	6	2	2	4	3	3	11	9
	April	5	2	2	4	3	3	10	9
	May	6	2	2	4	3	3	11	9

Source: Corpo de Fuzileiros, Unpublished History of the *Corpo de Fuzileiros, Part II: Fuzileiros Especiais* [Marine Corps, Part II: Special Marines], TMs [photocopy] (Lisbon: Ministério da Marinha, 1987), p.17; and Luís Sanches de Baêna, *Fuzileiros: Factos e Feitos na Guerra de* África *1961/1974*, Volume 1 [Fuzileiros: Facts and Feats in the African War 1961/1974, Volume 1] (Lisbon: Comissão Cultural da Marinha, 2006), pp.101–107.

Table 2

Naval Disposition (units of fuzileiros), 1961–1974

Units of Fuzileiros Deployed in the Naval Command of Angola

Units		Dates	
Type	Designation	Deployed	Redeployed
Detachments *(destacamentos de fuzileiros especiais)*	DFE 1	10 NOV 61	14 JUL 63
	DFE 3	29 AUG 62	23 NOV 64
	DFE 4	26 FEB 63	19 MAR 65
	DFE 5	21 JUN 63	15 JUL 65
	DFE 6	30 SEP 63	23 OCT 65
	DFE 11	14 NOV 64	06 DEC 66
	DFE 2	10 JUL 65	24 JUN 67
	DFE 13	23 OCT 65	15 SEP 67
	DFE 11	21 JUN 67	26 JUN 69
	DFE 2	21 AUG 67	05 NOV 69
	DFE 10	14 MAY 69	25 MAR 71
	DFE 1	27 JUL 69	06 OCT 71
	DFE 6	14 MAR 71	07 MAR 73
	DFE 10	04 OCT 71	06 NOV 73
	DFE 2	16 MAR 73	15 FEB 75
	DFE 6	09 OCT 73	27 MAR 75
	DFE 1	17 JUL 75	10 NOV 75
Companies *(companhias de fuzileiros)*	CF 1	31 MAY 62	06 JUN 64
	CF 4	01 JUN 64	09 JUN 66
	CF 5	10 NOV 64	29 DEC 66
	CF 10	08 JUN 66	05 AUG 68
	CF 1	02 DEC 66	19 JAN 69
	CF 11	17 DEC 66	24 JAN 69
	CF 7	04 AUG 68	24 JUL 70
	CF 5	05 AUG 68	06 SEP 70
	CF 8	31 DEC 68	08 DEC 70
	CF 9	17 JAN 69	08 FEB 71
	CF 4	19 JUL 70	10 JUL 72
	CF 6	31 AUG 70	06 AUG 72
	CF 7	07 DEC 70	28 NOV 72
	CF 5	30 JAN 71	23 JAN 73
	CF 1	10 JUL 72	06 JUN 74
	CF 3	06 AUG 72	13 SEP 74
	CF 4	28 NOV 72	17 DEC 74
	CF 6	09 JAN 73	21 JAN 75
	CF 8	29 JUN 74	21 APR 75
	CF 12	04 DEC 74	10 NOV 75
	CF 5	21 JAN 75	10 NOV 75
	CF 9	09 SEP 75	10 NOV 75

Source: Corpo de Fuzileiros, Unpublished History of the *Corpo de Fuzileiros, Part II: Fuzileiros Especiais* [Marine Corps, Part II: Special Marines], TMs [photocopy] (Lisbon: Ministério da Marinha, 1987), p.17; Luís Sanches de Baêna, *Fuzileiros: Factos e Feitos na Guerra de África 1961/1974*, Volume 1 [Fuzileiros: Facts and Feats in the African War 1961/1974, Volume 1] (Lisbon: Comissão Cultural da Marinha, 2006), pp.101–107.

Table 3

Disposition (units of fuzileiros), 1961–1974

Units of Fuzileiros Deployed in the Maritime Defence Command of Guiné

Units		Dates		Comments
Type	**Designation**	**Deployed**	**Redeployed**	
Detachments *(destacamentos de fuzileiros especiais)*	DFE 2	06 JUN 62	25 JUN 64	
	DFE 7	10 OCT 63	23 AUG 65	
	DFE 8	04 NOV 63	23 OCT 65	
	DFE 9	27 FEB 64	09 FEB 66	
	DFE 10	23 JUN 64	14 JUN 66	
	DFE 3	23 AUG 65	11 MAY 67	
	DFE 4	21 OCT 65	28 JUL 67	
	DFE 6	05 FEB 66	05 NOV 67	
	DFE 7	11 JUN 66	23 APR 68	
	DFE 10	10 MAY 67	09 MAR 69	
	DFE 3	25 JUL 67	19 APR 69	
	DFE 12	02 NOV 67	15 OCT 69	
	DFE 13	21 APR 68	25 JAN 70	
	DFE 7	20 FEB 69	16 SEP 70	
	DFE 8	19 APR 69	16 FEB 71	
	DFE 3	13 OCT 69	12 JUL 71	
	DFE 12	31 JAN 70	02 DEC 71	Relieved by DFE 22
	DFE 21★	21 APR 70		Deactivated 25 AUG 74
	DFE 4	14 SEP 70	24 JUN 72	
	DFE 13	22 JAN 71	20 OCT 72	
	DFE 8	09 JUL 71	12 APR 73	
	DFE 22★	16 NOV 71		Deactivated 25 AUG 74
	DFE 12	07 JUN 72	05 APR 74	
	DFE 1	06 OCT 72	28 JUL 74	
	DFE 4	07 APR 73	15 OCT 74	
	DFE 5	09 FEB 74	30 OCT 74	
	DFE 23★	01 JUL 74		Deactivated 25 AUG 74
Companies *(companhias de fuzileiros)*	PF 1	09 APR 63	14 JUN 63	
	CF 3	14 JUN 63	12 JUL 65	PF 1 absorbed by CF 3
	CF 7	08 JUL 65	11 MAY 67	
	CF 9	02 AUG 66	09 MAY68	
	CF 3	10 MAY 67	21 FEB 69	
	CF 6	06 MAY 68	01 FEB 70	
	CF 10	20 FEB 69	12 JAN 71	
	CF 3	31 JAN 70	02 DEC 71	
	CF 11	09 JAN 71	06 OCT 72	
	CF 8	24 NOV 71	23 AUG 73	
	CF 2	06 OCT 72	11 JUL 74	
	CF 5	23 AUG 73	03 OCT 74	

★African detachments of special fuzileiros.

Source: Corpo de Fuzileiros, Unpublished History of the *Corpo de Fuzileiros, Part II: Fuzileiros Especiais* [Marine Corps, Part II: Special Marines], TMs [photocopy] (Lisbon: Ministério da Marinha, 1987), p.17; Luís Sanches de Baêna, *Fuzileiros: Factos e Feitos na Guerra de África 1961/1974*, Volume 1 [Fuzileiros: Facts and Feats in the African War 1961/1974, Volume 1] (Lisbon: Comissão Cultural da Marinha, 2006), pp.101–107.

Table 4

Disposition (units of fuzileiros), 1961–1974

Units of Fuzileiros Deployed in the Naval Command of Mozambique

Units		Dates	
Type	**Designation**	**Deployed**	**Redeployed**
Detachments *(destacamentos de fuzileiros especiais)*	DFE 1	20 NOV 64	01 DEC 66
	DFE 12	20 JUN 65	30 JUN 67
	DFE 5	27 NOV 65	09 NOV 67
	DFE 8	26 NOV 66	24 NOV 68
	DFE 9	24 FEB 67	28 MAR 69
	DFE 1	22 JUN 67	30 JUN 69
	DFE 4	05 NOV 67	29 NOV 69
	DFE 6	05 NOV 68	06 SEP 70
	DFE 5	01 MAR 69	10 FEB 71
	DFE 9	17 JUN 69	24 JUL 71
	DFE 11	16 NOV 69	18 JAN 72
	DFE 2	24 AUG 70	10 MAY 72
	DFE 7	08 FEB 71	06 NOV 72
	DFE 5	18 JUL 71	13 APR 73
	DFE 9	22 DEC 71	03 DEC 73
	DFE 3	03 MAY 72	20 MAY 74
	DFE 11	01 NOV 72	01 NOV 74
	DFE 8	03 DEC 73	03 DEC 74
	DFE 10	13 MAY 74	24 JUN 75
Companies *(companhias de fuzileiros)*	CF 2	29 OCT 62	25 MAR 65
	CF 6	19 MAR 65	18 MAY 67
	CF 8	27 NOV 65	28 FEB 68
	CF 2	02 MAY 67	15 JUN 69
	CF 4	16 FEB 68	06 MAR 70
	CF 1	13 JUN 69	01 JUN 71
	CF 2	21 FEB 70	18 JAN 72
	CF 10	01 JUN 71	07 MAY 73
	CF 9	18 JAN 72	14 JAN 74
	CF 11	06 APR 73	08 NOV 74
	CF 7	07 MAY 73	22 NOV 74
	CF 10	14 JAN 74	★ 75

★ Principally in JUN.

Source: Corpo de Fuzileiros, Unpublished History of the *Corpo de Fuzileiros, Part II: Fuzileiros Especiais* [Marine Corps, Part II: Special Marines], TMs [photocopy] (Lisbon: Ministério da Marinha, 1987), p.17; Luís Sanches de Baêna, *Fuzileiros: Factos e Feitos na Guerra de África 1961/1974*, Volume 1 [Fuzileiros: Facts and Feats in the African War 1961/1974, Volume 1] (Lisbon: Comissão Cultural da Marinha, 2006), pp.101–107.

(Endnotes)

1. Marcello Caetano, "Editorial," *O Mundo Português* [Portuguese World], 2 (1935), p.218.

2. A. de Roboredo (*capitão de mar e guerra*), Estado-Maior da Armada, to Jaime Lopes (*capitão de fragata*), Naval Aide, Embassy of Portugal, London, 3 February 1959, memorandum "instrucão de 'comandos'," Coloredo Box 224/2082, Arquivo Central da Marinha, Antiga Fabrica Nacional de Cordoaria, Rua da Junqueira, Lisbon, p.1.

3. António José Malheiro García, "Particiação da Armada na Defesa das Provincias Ultramarinas, Actividade Oceânica, Breve Retrospectiva da Actividade Naval na Década de 50" [Participation of the Navy in the Defense of the Overseas Provinces, Oceanic Role, Retrospective Brief of the Naval Role in the Decade of the 50s], in the unpublished collection *Participação da Armada na Defesa das Províncias Ultramarinas* [Participation of the Navy in the Defense of the Overseas Provinces], TMs [photocopy] (Lisbon: Ministério de Marinha 1972), p.3.

4. António José Telo, *História da Marinha Portuguesa: Doutrinas e Organização, 1924–1974* [History of the Portuguese Navy: Doctrine and Organization, 1924–1974] (Lisbon: Academia de Marinha, 1999), p.536.

5. Ibid.

6. Thomas J. Cutler, *Brown Water, Black Berets* (Annapolis: Naval Institute Press, 1988), p.153.

7. The first eight vessels in the class were: *Bellatrix* (P 363), *Canopus* (P 364), *Deneb* (P 365), *Espiga* (P 366), *Fomalhaut* (P 367), *Pollux* (P 368), *Altair* (P 377) and *Rigel* (P 378). The final five vessels were: *Arcturus* (P 1151), *Aldebaran* (P 1152), *Procion* (P 1153), *Sirus* (P 1154) and *Vega* (P 1155).

8. John P. Cann, *Brown Waters of Africa: Portuguese Riverine Warfare, 1961–1974* (Solihull, United Kingdom: Helion & Company, 2013), p.76.

9. Telo, *História da Marinha Portuguesa,* p. 558. One commercial firm buying in the United States on behalf of the Portuguese Navy was Progresso, Lda.

10. Ibid.

11. *Comandante* is a title conferred on all Portuguese naval commanding officers, regardless of rank, and to all officers with the rank of Lieutenant Commander and above. There is no equivalent in English.

12. Telo, *História da Marinha Portuguesa,* footnote 70, p.559.

13. Estado-Maior da Armada, IV Divisão, *Características Principais das Novas Unidades Navais e do Material das Unidades de Fuzileiros* [Principal Characteristics of New Naval and Marine Units] (Lisbon: Estado-Maior da Armada, December 1969), pp.5–6.

14. A. de Roboredo (*almirante*), Chefe Estado-Maior da Armada, to Minister of the Navy, Lisbon, 14 December 1964, memorandum "Lanchas de Disembarque" [Landing Craft], Coloredo Box 224/601, Arquivo Central da Marinha, Antiga Fabrica Nacional de Cordoaria, Rua da Junqueira, Lisbon.

15. There were four of the LDG 100 series: *Alfange* (LDG 101), *Aríete* (LGD 102), *Cimitarra* (LDG 103) and *Montante* (LDG 104). There were two of the LDG 200 series: *Bombarda* (LDG 105), later re-designated LDG 201, and *Albarda* (LDG 202).

16. Cann, *Brown Waters of Africa*, p.78.

17. Telo, *História da Marinha Portuguesa,* footnote 71, p.559.

18. A.B. Rodrigues da Costa, "As Lanchas de Desembarque da Classe *Alfange* (1965–1975)" [*Alfange* Class Landing Craft (1965–1975)], *Revista da Armada* (November 1996): 11; João Falcão de Campos, "Armada Portuguesa: Lanchas e Navios" [Portuguese Navy: Boats and Ships] in *Guerra Colonial* [Colonial War], eds. Aniceto Afonso and Carlos de Matos Gomes (Lisbon: Editorial Notícias, 2000), p.389.

19. Ibid., p.13.

20. Ibid., p.10.

21. Turíbio Abreu, "O Bote de Borracha" [The Rubber Boat], *Anais do Clube Militar Naval* (July-September 1967): p.603. While the boats could accommodate outboard engines greater than 35 horsepower, this limit was imposed to contain maintenance costs with acceptable sacrifice in speed.

22. Ibid.

23. Telo, *História da Marinha Portuguesa*, p.543.

24. Armando de Roboredo, "Marinha de Guerra Portuguesa na actual conjuntura" [The Portuguese Navy Meeting Current Challenges], *Anais do Clube Militar Naval* (July–September 1965), p.480.

25. Ibid.

26. Estado-Maior do Exército (EME), *Resenha Histórico-Militar das Campanhas de África (1961–1974)* [Historical-Military Report on the African Campaigns (1961–1974)] (Lisbon: Estado-Maior do Exército, 1989), Vol. II, pp.19–20; and A. Teixeira da Mota, *Guiné Portuguesa* [Portuguese Guiné] (Lisbon: Agência Geral do Ultramar, 1954), p.128. Only the navigable river distances are used in the calculations, as coastal security was not a significant factor in either Angola (Atlantic Ocean) or Mozambique (Indian Ocean) because of the lack of insurgent seaborne capability and the distance of any fighting from these coasts. Insurgents could and did cross non-navigable sections, which in Angola, Guiné and Mozambique were substantial, but it was not practicable to establish waterborne river patrols on these bodies because of shallow depths, narrow widths, or rapids.

27. *Jane's Fighting Ships 1946-47* (London: Sampson Low, Marston & Co., 1947), pp.252–258.

28. *Jane's Fighting Ships 1960-1961* (London: Jane's Fighting Ships Publishing Co., 1961), pp.251–256.

29. *Fighting Ships 1974-75* (London: Jane's Yearbooks, 1975), pp.267–274.

30. L.H. Gann, "Portugal, Africa, and the Future," *Journal of Modern African Studies* (March 1975), pp.2–3.

31. John P. Cann, *Counterinsurgency in Africa* (Westport, Conn.: Greenwood Publishing, 1997), pp.6–7.

32. A. de Roboredo (*capitão de mar e guerra*), Estado-Maior da Armada, 5 May 1959, point paper "*Fuzileiros*," Coloredo Box 224/2082, Arquivo Central da Marinha, Antiga Fabrica Nacional de Cordoaria, Rua da Junqueira, Lisbon.

33. Jorge Semedo de Matos, "O Terço da Armada da Coroa de Portugal" [The Naval Regiment of the Portuguese Crown], *Revista da Armada* (June 1999), pp.10–11.

34. A total of 1,770 men.

35. A total of 2,124 men. A company of fuzileiros was composed of one captain (*capitão*), one first lieutenant (*tenente*), one second lieutenant (*alferes*), four sergeants (*sargentos*), one storekeeper (*furrier*), two squad corporals (*cabos de esquadra*), one drummer (*tambor*) and 160 fuzileiros.

36. A total of 1,328 men. There were nine companies of artificers with 132 men each and one company of ballasters with 148 men.

37. Carlos Lorch, ed., *Fuzileiros Navais, Brazil's Amphibious Warriors* (Rio de Janeiro: Action Editora, 1997), pp.34–36.

38.   Each company was composed of one captain (*capitão*), one first lieutenant (*tenente*), one second lieutenant (*alferes*), one staff sergeant (*primeiro sargento*), four sergeants (*sargentos*), two drummers (*tambores*), eight corporals (*cabos*) and 92 privates (*soldados*).

39.   Each company was composed of one captain (*capitão*), one first lieutenant (*tenente*), one second lieutenant (*alferes*), one staff sergeant (*primeiro sargento*), one storekeeper (*furrier*), five corporals (*cabos*), five lance corporals (*anspeçadas*), 64 privates (*soldados*) and one bugler (*corneta*).

40.   Telo, *História da Marinha Portuguesa*, p.550.

41.   Comando Naval de Angola to Estado-Maior da Armada, Luanda, 11 April 1960, Nota № 28 "Segurança das provincias ultramarinas," Coloredo Box Angola/176, Arquivo Central da Marinha, Antiga Fabrica Nacional de Cordoaria, Rua da Junqueira, Lisbon.

42.   Jorge Alexandre da Fonseca (*tenente coronel*), Military and Aeronautical Attaché, Embassy of Portugal in Paris, to A. de Roboredo (*capitão de mar e guerra*), Estado-Maior da Armada, Paris, 3 February 1959, memorandum "Relaying approval for the training of 1 *lieutenant de vaisseau*, 1 *sous-officer* et 5 *marins* at the École *des Fusiliers*, Centre Siroco, Algeria," Coloredo Box 224/2082, Arquivo Central da Marinha, Antiga Fabrica Nacional de Cordoaria, Rua da Junqueira, Lisbon.

43.   A. de Roboredo (*capitão de mar e guerra*), Estado-Maior da Armada, to Naval Attaché, Embassy of Portugal in London, 3 February 1959, memorandum "Primary request for training a group," Coloredo Box 224/2082, Arquivo Central da Marinha, Antiga Fabrica Nacional de Cordoaria, Rua da Junqueira, Lisbon; and Jaime Lopes (*capitão de fragata*), Naval Attaché, Embassy of Portugal in London, to Estado-Maior da Armada, London, 3 April 1959, memorandum "Instruction of 'Commandos'," Coloredo Box 224/2082, Arquivo Central da Marinha, Antiga Fabrica Nacional de Cordoaria, Rua da Junqueira, Lisbon.

44.   António Alves Leite (*contra almirante*), Sub-chefe do Estado-Maior da Armada, to Chefe do Estado-Maior da Armada, Lisbon, 1 May 1959, memorandum "Instrução de commandos," Coloredo Box 224/2082, Arquivo Central da Marinha, Antiga Fabrica Nacional de Cordoaria, Rua da Junqueira, Lisbon.

45.   Luís Celestino da Silva (*contra almirante*), Superintendência dos Servios da Armada, to Estado-Maior da Armada, Lisbon, 6 June 1960, memorandum "Instrução de 'comandos'," Coloredo Box 224/601, Arquivo Central da Marinha, Antiga Fabrica Nacional de Cordoaria, Rua da Junqueira, Lisbon.

46.   Decreto-Lei № 43515 of 24 February 1961.

47.   Escola de Fuzileiros. Portaria № 18509 of 3 June 1961.

48.   Portaria № 18774 of 13 October 1961.

49.   Corpo de Fuzileiros, *Part II: Fuzileiros Especiais*, Unpublished History (Lisbon: Ministério da Marinha, 1987), p.14.

50.   Rui Hortelão, Luís Sanches de Baêna, and Abel Melo e Sousa, *Alpoim Calvão: Honra e Dever* [Alpoim Calvão: Honor and Duty] (Porto: Caminhos Romanos, 2012), p.52. The air distance from Peniche to Vale de Zebro is 60 miles.

51.   Luís Sanches de Baêna, *Fuzileiros: Factos e Feitos na Guerra de* África *1961/1974*, Vol. 1 [*Fuzileiros*: Facts and Feats in the African War 1961/1974, Vol. 1] (Lisbon: Comissão Cultural da Marinha, 2006), p.46.

52.   Ibid., p.48.

53.   Capitão de fragata Luís Jorge Matos, interview with the author, 10 February 2003, Bélem.

54.   "Fuzileiros" draft article, TMs [photocopy], *Diário de Notícas*, 1995, p.3.

55.   Ibid.

CHAPTER 2
THE NORTH OF ANGOLA

European troop strength in Angola numbered under 1,000 in early 1958, and was reinforced only to about 3,000 by mid-1960.[1] Overall strength was 8,000, of which at least 5,000 were African troops.[2] These forces, while scattered throughout Angola, were confined to garrisons in the larger towns and accustomed merely to administering subjective rule.[3] This modest order of battle was neither properly organized, nor trained, nor led – and its numbers were inadequate to face the uprisings in early 1961.

On 15 March 1961, the UPA – in an almost indescribably primordial fashion – attacked across a 300-kilometer strip into the north-west border area of Angola and penetrated into the Dembos region, an area of rugged terrain and relatively isolated settlements and coffee farms. The concentrated assault of an estimated 5,000 UPA forces and the forced recruiting of perhaps another 25,000 overwhelmed local authorities and left the area paralyzed.[4] Several thousand whites, blacks and *mestiços* were brutally and grotesquely murdered in an unimaginable fashion over the next several weeks. Villages, towns, outposts and farms were overrun, and the looting and destruction of property became a trademark of the mayhem. While the UPA quickly

reached its culmination point, there remained thousands of attackers roaming about Northern Angola searching for food and committing atrocities with precious few Portuguese resources available to round them up and restore order. All of Portugal was shocked at the horror,

A coffee plantation, north of Angola.
(Source: Estado-Maior da Armada and *Revista da Armada*)

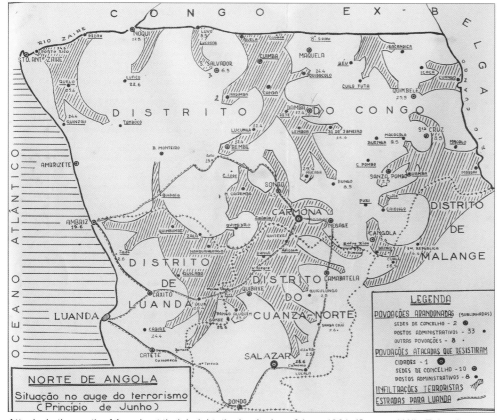

Attacks in the north of Angola at their height: the beginning of June 1961. (Source: Hélio Felgas)

that such lawlessness should be tolerated, and a strong, uncompromising reaction to the nationalist behaviour was widely supported.

With this assault and the ensuing chaos, there was simply not enough manpower (skilled or not) to address the upheaval. A patchwork of civil-military defense was cobbled together to halt the UPA advance, kill or capture the perpetrators and address the grave civil distress. The navy was drawn into this vacuum, and the importance of its small contribution of little more than 450 men proved to be disproportionate, despite the many non-traditional roles. Its personnel benefited from their discipline, training, skilled leadership and particularly the secure waterborne mobility that bypassed the rudimentary and vulnerable infrastructure.[8] While the deployment of detachments ashore from each ship's company would reduce shipboard manning by perhaps a quarter of the normal complement, each vessel continued to execute its assignment and relied on the personal sacrifice of the remaining crewmen on board and the longer days and extra duties that it implied.[9] It was thus into this temporary breech that the small but stout-hearted naval presence was immediately thrown and proceeded to distinguish itself.

The naval force initially concentrated its resources on policing the 80-mile Zaire River Frontier from Noqui, where the river crosses the Angola-Congo border, all the way to the Atlantic Ocean. It was further responsible for maritime security along the Angolan Coastline in the Atlantic from Lake Massábi in the enclave of Cabinda to the Cunene River on the border with South-West Africa. The tasks varied from landing detachments of sailors to act in an infantry role, to performing relief operations, to transporting troops, to patrolling waterways as a reassuring presence – all in coordination with the sister services. This action clearly demonstrated a need for naval power projection ashore, and its initial detachments of fuzileiros were to appear shortly.

An Amazing Land

Angola is a vast territory of 1,246,314 square kilometers – an area that is about 14 times the size of Portugal, or as large as the combined areas of Spain, France and Italy. Its land frontier, with its neighbors of the former Belgian Congo (Zaire), Northern Rhodesia (Zambia) and South-West Africa (Namibia) extends 4,837 kilometers and is so lengthy and remote that it is virtually impossible to control. The Zaire River, which comprises a relatively small 80-mile part of the border in the north-west, remains full of thickly-wooded islands that provided excellent cover for insurgents. The frontier was long and difficult, and the Portuguese crews small – thus despite its average

and Roberto's belief that Portugal would act as Belgium did and grant independence in the face of extreme violence proved false.

This savage foray occurred in an area demarcated by the Congolese Frontier, the Cuango River, the Malange-Luanda Railroad and the Atlantic Ocean. The attackers pushed nearly to Luanda (the capital). Military leaders faced a situation in which over 100 administrative posts and towns in the three districts of Northern Angola from the Congo border to within 30 miles of Luanda had been either wiped out, taken, or paralyzed by the UPA. Over 1,000 Europeans and an unknown number of Africans were thought to have perished, and the economy of Northern Angola was crippled. Communications were largely cut or damaged. Finally, thousands of Portuguese refugees were camped in Luanda, or on their way back to Portugal. The chaotic internal situation in Angola was rapidly and sensationally projected to a large international audience over the succeeding several months.[5]

For a month, Portugal and Angola seemed paralyzed and unable to act. Equally, the insurgents were incapable of sustained military engagement. Civil militias were formed, and loyal Africans armed. It was this patchwork of civil-military defense and its frenetic activity that brought UPA momentum to a halt. Formal military reoccupation began on 13 May and was intensified as troops arrived from the *metrópole*. During the July/August period, approximately 20,000 reinforcements landed in Angola, and because of the fighting over 150,000 refugees fled the area over the next nine months, mostly to the Congo.[6] Later it was estimated that about 500 Europeans and 20,000 local people died in this *jacquerie*.[7] It deeply shocked all of Portugal and hardened the colonial commitment. The restoration of order in Angola became the focus of a nation. To the Portuguese, it was unthinkable current of 4.5 knots, crossings could be and were made undetected at virtually any point. Its average width of about 1.5 kilometers was hardly an impediment.[10] The terrain from the border southward remains likewise covered with dense tropical forest originating in the riverbanks of the Zaire, which gives way to thick elephant grass eight to 10 feet tall, swamp and mountain. This region shelters diverse fauna such as crocodiles, elephants, deer and *paçaças* (or Angolan buffalos). The few roads through the area were beaten earth and were little better than tracks.

Angola is also a land of geographical contrasts: topographically, it is bordered on the west by the Atlantic Ocean, where a coastal belt runs the length of the approximately 1,650-kilometer shoreline, rising to a central highland 50 to 200 kilometers inland that covers about 60 percent of the country. This highland varies in altitude between 1,000 meters and its highest point of 2,619 meters at Môca, a mount in the district of Huambo. Further inland, the land descends to an eastern plateau with an elevation as high as 1,600 meters.

The diversity of relief and the territorial extent of Angola produce a varied climate ranging from tropical wet in the Dembos region, to mild wet in the northern coastal plains, to tropical dry in the southern highlands, to semi-desert in the south-east. The rainy season occurs between November and May and is followed by a form of winter, known locally as the *cacimbo* (or drizzle season), which extends to November.

Such vastness and diversity in terrain have always made communication difficult in Angola. This difficulty would extend to both the insurgents and government forces, and each would find its solution in very different ways. From external sanctuaries the insurgents would struggle over long and difficult passages to reach local populations that could be proselytized and tapped for food, shelter, recruits and intelligence. On the other hand, the Portuguese would protect these populations by isolating the insurgents within the vastness of the country and destroying them with military force. In support of this strategy, the navy began its operations along the coast and moved into the rivers, as the fight matured. It began with a very small force and expanded it into a large and very effective riverine navy of fuzileiros and their small boats that provided them with their mobility.

Mopping-up operations became more robust from June onward, as army troops were mobilized in the *metrópole* and began arriving by ship in Luanda. The navy redirected its resources toward the towns

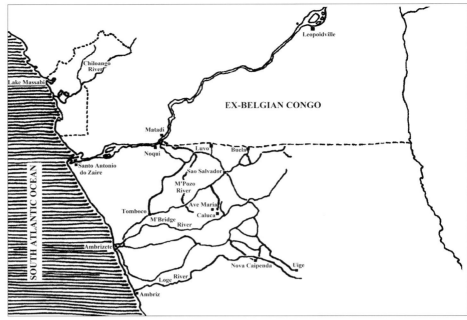
Northern Angola's initial operating areas. (Source: the author)

DFE 1 landing at Moçâmedes in December 1961 as part of its publicity exercise. (Source: Estado-Maior da Armada and *Revista da Armada*)

The launch *Lué* on the Chiloango River in Cabinda. (Source: Estado-Maior da Armada and *Revista da Armada*)

of Noqui and Santo António do Zaire along the Zaire River, and to Landana in the enclave of Cabinda, although it was not threatened at the time, and the navy acted more like a ferry service around Lake Massábi and along the Chiloango River with its small launch *Lué*.

For the navy, however, the 80-mile Zairian riverine border was the center of activity during the initial years of the conflict. While its action began on the coast with a modest force, it soon moved into this grand river as rapidly as resources arrived – and experience was gained in projecting power and securing the frontier from infiltration. Defensively, the navy established static posts at key points along the Zaire from which it could project power. These posts were essentially fuzileiro bases. Offensively, it conducted patrols continuously along the riverine frontier.

Fuzileiros operating in the north of Angola with other land forces. (Source: Estado-Maior da Armada and *Revista da Armada*)

Arrival of the Fuzileiros

In addition to the arrival of the '30-tonners', the Naval Command of Angola had been expecting its first detachment of special fuzileiros during the second half of October 1961 to help alleviate the burden on the crews of its ships in acting as infantry ashore.[11] The initial thought was that the expected detachment would establish itself at a base near its anticipated area of operations, so that it could become familiar with its operating environment. The unit, after all, would be arriving fresh from its training in the *metrópole*. While its fuzileiros would be skilled in the traditional techniques, tactics and procedures of their tradecraft, they would not have acquired a familiarity with the local terrain and operating conditions that would give them an advantage over (or at least an equal footing) with the enemy in the Zairian surroundings. This period of adaptation to Africa was an important part of the fuzileiro acclimation process.

Detachment of Special Fuzileiros No. 1 (DFE 1) finally arrived by air on 10 and 15 November and the following week boarded the frigates *Diogo Gomes* and *Pero Escobar* to exercise in the south along the littoral and far from the area where they were needed most. Prior to boarding the ships, the lieutenant commanding the detachment gave a patriotic and rousing address to his troops, and as they marched up the gangway to the tune 'Angola is Ours', there was not a dry eye in the crowd of spectators.

During the early days of December, the fuzileiros made landings in Moçâmedes, Bengula and Novo Redondo, which were as much a display of the new naval force as an exercise to retain proficiency. In a publicity move rivaling that of the US Marine Corps, local newspapers were invited to witness the activity. Such events as an 'attack' on the Morena Beach and the 'occupation' of the Bengula Railway Station were reported with sober praise and portfolios of photographs.[12] While this excursion may have seemed almost frivolous in light of conditions that continued to exist in the north – and did delay the force from becoming immediately engaged there – the effect on civilian morale was uplifting and important in a time of enormous concern. It reinforced the fact that the government was taking charge of the situation and discharging its duty to protect the population.

At the conclusion of the several weeks of demonstrations, the detachment was moved to São Salvador for a period of two months,

where it participated in operations with other land forces in the neighboring region of Buela and in the area demarcated by São Salvador, Tombôco and the M'Pozo River, which ran between the two towns. It was subsequently used to inspect traffic and patrol along the coast north of Luanda, along the lines of infiltration across the Zaire River and along the margins of the Chiloango River and Lake Massábi within the Cabinda enclave. The detachment also operated from time to time with army elements supporting various sector commanders as reserve forces, or laying ambushes and executing surprise attacks as a part of various coordinated plans. These occurred largely along the Ambriz-Ambrizete axis and around the small settlements (or *sanzalas*) of Caluca and Avé Maria near the M'Bridge River (variously Mebridege or Mebridge) south of São Salvador in the difficult terrain of the Dembos region.

Fuzileiro José Talhadas, who operated in the Dembos with DFE 2, described conditions there:

> I was in the Dembos where I learned that a prolonged silence in the bush was an indication that there were others present, the scene of an ambush, that a cry in the night carried dozens of kilometers, that any negligence ended human survival, and that any laxness could result in the death of the comrade in front or behind me.[13]

Indeed, the Dembos was a place of luxuriant vegetation, dense forest, tall trees and surprisingly uneven terrain with elevated hills – and all of this was accompanied by an overwhelming humidity that made everyone sweat profusely. Talhadas describes his camouflage fatigue jacket being soaked as if he had just washed it.[14] Following the arrival of Company of Fuzileiros No. 1 (CF 1) in May and Detachment of Special Fuzileiros No. 3 (DFE 3) in August 1962, the fuzileiros would undertake more ambitious actions. Before these could occur, however, there needed to be a broader plan for security on the Zaire…

Posts Along The Zaire

As the second year of the war opened, it became obvious that while the political situation in the Congo was unsettled and fluid, the enemy

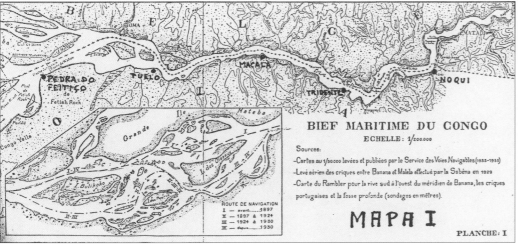

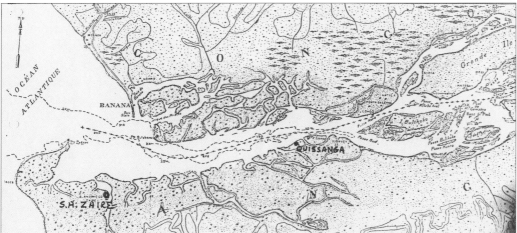

A Belgian chart of the Zaire River between Noqui and Santo António do Zaire. It was used by the Portuguese Navy from March 1961 and annotated by the user to show the location of the new naval posts established during the initial years of the conflict. (Source: Estado-Maior da Armada and *Revista da Armada*)

constantly in cooperation first with paratroops around the devastated village of Nova Caipemba (about 150 kilometers south of São Salvador on the Loge River) and then with army units on the Plaines de Congo Yella south and west of Fetish Rock on the Zaire, where it constructed a riverine post.[16] Later after the arrival on 23 September 1961 of the patrol launches *Espiga*, *Fomalhaut* and *Pollux*, the DFE was able to begin regular patrolling along the Zaire in areas with the obscure names of Bulicoco Island, Quissanga, Lucala, Quibembe, Chichianga, Ponta Puela and the Zaire tributary of Lué Pequeno (next to Noqui) joining the newly-initiated launch operations. It soon became clear that the small force in place, no matter how excellent, could not control the riverine border adequately to prevent enemy infiltration nearly at will.

Additional resources began to arrive early in the New Year and were projected to continue to do so throughout 1962. Three new launches – *Altair*, *Rigel* and *Régulus*

had made good use of his sanctuary and now was better armed, more aggressive and increasingly well organized. He was reappearing in force in areas that were thought to be pacified and making a concerted effort to expand his presence not only in the border areas, but also in the interior of the country. His main lines of infiltration from the naval perspective were across the Zaire River first at Ponta Puelo (approximately opposite the Congolese city of Boma) and later in May near the more isolated Bulicoco Island and its islets further downstream.[15] Both of these areas were characterized by a myriad of small islands and thick undergrowth that provided excellent cover for insurgents seeking to cross undetected. The migration north into the Congo had left the north-east largely depopulated, and as relative peace returned, the displaced too began to return in a steady trickle. These returnees had in many cases been recruited by the UPA and often accompanied the insurgents to help them find their way and to give them credibility with the local population. The fact remained, however, that there was little population in the north to provide them with the all-important support that they required, and thus these efforts made little immediate impact. Nevertheless, as the situation became increasingly stable and more attractive to refugees in the Congo, and as these citizens began to return in significant numbers, the navy anticipated an increasing security problem.

From the beginning of the New Year, DFE 1 had operated almost

– were welcomed on 20 February, and there was by late spring a sense of urgency within the navy to develop a strategic plan for effective security on the Zaire to complement the land frontiers and to deploy its expanding forces to achieve this end.

The original concept called for increased vigilance along the river supported by a series of small forts (or *fortins*) located at judicious intervals to establish a strong barrier to insurgent infiltration. By mid-month, the plan *Dispositivo Detentor* (Deterrent Force) had been proposed for the eastern fluvial boundary with the Congo – the area of greatest riverine infiltration – and called for fixed posts to be established at dominant points between Noqui and Fetish Rock. The logic in choosing these initial locations was that they would divide this stretch of river into approximately four equal parts, with an average of 7.5 miles between them. This division would facilitate the formation of patrol zones around each post and would equally apportion the potential surveillance workload. Later, a fourth post would be proposed and established on the island of Quissanga, from which fuzileiros were already operating in their rubber boats and being billeted in an abandoned sawmill that was flooded by the river from time to time. The posts were designed as the static logistic skeleton on which would rest the dynamic muscle of the fuzileiros and launches. The plan had the flexibility for expansion and was built on the assumption that additional troops, launches and larger vessels

The post of Quissanga in September 1965.
(Source: Estado-Maior da Armada and *Revista da Armada*)

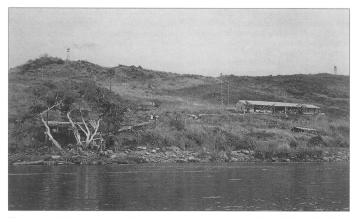

The post of Macala; note the twin lookout towers on the hilltops (left and right) and the pier (lower-left).
(Source: Estado-Maior da Armada and *Revista da Armada*)

would become available to tighten frontier security.[17] Initially, each post would have two sections of fuzileiros (or about 24 men), two sergeants and an officer; however, these numbers would change as conditions changed.[18] The numbers of DFEs in Angola built to four by September 1963, and as conditions on the Zaire improved, they were transferred to other areas where they could be more productively deployed. The number declined in March 1965 to three and then to two in December 1966 until the end of the conflict.

Planning work began on the bases with army support in June 1962, and by July, actual site excavation and construction were progressing. The task of carving four support bases from the virgin wilderness of the riverbanks was daunting in its difficulty, particularly with the limited labor available. Land had to be cleared of underbrush, and large stones removed by hand in the grading process. Building material then had to be landed on the riverbank in each case and moved to the construction sites. Each post consisted of a small headquarters building that was prefabricated from wood. It was constructed in the form of a pavilion and contained a command post, a mess, a radio station, officer quarters and enlisted barracks. There was also separately on each post a kitchen, sanitary facilities, a small magazine and armory, a lookout tower, a pier and a shelter for the rubber boats and their motors. Vegetable gardens were traditionally planted, and sources of potable water located. All of this was surrounded with concertinas of barbed wire for security.[19] The fuzileiro in this case was everything: combatant, carpenter, mason and farmer. He did it all.[20]

Talhadas, who served on the Zaire at the time, described the appearance of these posts:

> The posts, constructed of wood, in practice, were indistinguishable from the wood and thatch huts of the native population. There was little difference from the small village nearby; it was not less grubby, but our men did not present the tattered appearance of their neighboring locals. In fact, all of us used the military uniform, which in reality was not worn in the day-to-day activities at the post and in the conduct of patrols, as we were in the midst of a tropical climate, and to be clothed permanently from head to foot was absurd.[21]

This feverish activity resulted in the first post being completed at Puelo in mid-August. Macala was finished by the end of September and Quissanga by the first week of December. Trident (the final post) was completed three days before Christmas, and the system between Fetish Rock and Noqui now had the potential to tighten the riverine frontier.

At the same time, arrangements for the logistical support of this base structure were under way. The ready source of electrical power at the naval radio stations of Luanda and Santo António do Zaire translated into handsome cold storage facilities at both, but moving the chilled victuals to the posts presented a problem. Unfortunately, there were too few available resources. This situation put severe strain on all naval vessels, but particularly on the scarce landing craft that were in high demand to move troops and their equipment for military operations. It also presented other problems, as cold storage on both the landing craft and the launches was limited or non-existent. This meant that schedules had to be adjusted to move the perishable supplies in the coolness of the night to prevent spoilage. The first small landing craft (LDP 105) did not arrive until March 1963. Prior to that time, the launches struggled to carry the needed supplies in addition to their normal loads of fuzileiros, rubber boats, sacks of mail, outboard motors, fuel, spare parts and all of the other necessities for an isolated post. This initial, but temporary, solution was very impractical.[22] As time passed, conditions on the posts improved from their rudimentary nature to a more civilized and agreeable one. Native cooking was introduced, and this development was welcomed by both the post personnel and the launch crews.[23]

In October 1962, during the midst of the post construction when manpower was at a premium, military operations increased. Elements from the expanded force of fuzileiros combined with elements of Cavalry Battalion 345 and Parachute Battalion 21 to perform the first helicopter assaults of the war with Operation *'Parafuso Grande'* ('Large Screw'). Sixteen parachutists were airlifted in four Alouette II helicopters in a successful hammer and anvil operation culminating in the destruction of the UPA base at Caluca, which was in the midst of the area affected by the UPA attacks.[24]

Laster in December of the same year, Operation *'Ferrolho'* ('Rifle Bolt') began in which the fuzileiros – supported by the launches – ranged along the Zaire, sweeping the river between the strategic

A fuzileiro operation from Santo António do Zaire; note the effects of heat on uniform formality. (Source: Anne Gaüzes and Dante Vacchi)

A squad of fuzileiros launching from Santo António do Zaire. (Source: Anne Gaüzes and Dante Vacchi)

A squad of fuzileiros at Quissanga; note the officer on the left in shorts and a uniform shirt, with neither beret nor shoes, because of the heat. (Source: Personal archive of José Augusto Pires de Lima)

points of Quissanga, Fetish Rock, Puelo, Macala and Trident all the way to Noqui.[25] In addition to the obstacles in establishing the naval posts, the fuzileiros in their fragile rubber boats and the launch crews had to overcome an adverse operating environment and address not only a human enemy, but also a natural one. The Zaire itself was full of whirlpools (particularly opposite the post of Trident), giant tree trunks and branches, floating islands of grass and mud, and sharp rocks. Because of the flow and consequent change in the river, charts were rarely accurate. Nights on the river were opaquely black, and unannounced and violent rainstorms would drastically reduce the effectiveness of patrols.[26] Radar was a help, but vigilant lookouts were more useful in spotting floating obstacles and guiding vessels during shoreline operations. Further, the river contained a vast region of canals along an 11-mile stretch between Bulicoco Island (just east of Quissanga) and Fetish Rock, the most dangerous part of its length. The canals, which were estimated to total some 800 miles of waterway, ran between the numerous islands and small tributaries and proved to be ready-made enemy hiding places that were difficult to police.[27] The other islands, with their interesting animal names of 'Hippopotamus', 'Egret', 'Duck', 'Fish Hawk', 'Turtle', 'Hummingbird', 'Iguana', 'Tsetse' and so on also concealed the enemy in their thick brush.

Typical of fuzileiro operations during late 1962 was the October clearing of the many small islands and canals that compose the Bulicoco Archipelago. This complex covers an area of approximately 6,000 square meters – not particularly large, but one of the most complicated of any on the Zaire.[28] Quite naturally it attracted the enemy, as it provided excellent concealment and served as an ideal night-time launching site for his canoes to cross into Angola. Its interior was a labyrinth of narrow canals, whose twists, turns, forks and sandy shoals could easily lose troops. It was so complicated that even with a chart, it was easy to be lost. Its canals were also so shallow and narrow that only the rubber boats of the fuzileiros could penetrate them and negotiate the dense undergrowth along their banks, the foliage overhanging the water and the vines drooping from the verdant canopy. Even in daylight, these canals could be dark and often had the appearance of a tunnel or the interior of a ruined cathedral with the high jungle cover.

Fuzileiros operating in the canals of Bulicoco Island.
(Source: Estado-Maior da Armada and *Revista da Armada*)

A squad of fuzileiros conducting an operation from Quissanga, April 1967, in the canals of Bulicoco Island.
(Source: Estado-Maior da Armada and *Revista da Armada*)

Fuzileiros patrolling a canal in the Bulicoco Archipelago. The jungle canopy over the waterways gave them a cave-like darkness and made them ideal hiding places for insurgents. (Source: Escola de Fuzileiros)

Preparations for the operation were extensive – and for the first time, air reconnaissance in the form of an Auster was integrated into the plan to help guide the surface force through the waterway maze. The seasoned DFE 1 and the newly-arrived DFE 3 were the designated ground forces. The contrast between the worn and stained battle dress of the veteran unit and the neat and clean ones of the fresh arrivals was obvious, but belied the capabilities of the newcomers. These troops were transported to the area from Santo António do Zaire by the launches during the early hours of the morning and launched in their rubber boats opposite Bulicoco in the predawn at the extreme low tide. The fuzileiros began to explore the canal system inch by inch guided by the spotter aircraft. A number of empty encampments were discovered, searched and then destroyed. One boat of fuzileiros abruptly encountered two insurgents in a canoe at the close range of 30 meters, and both opened fire. The fuzileiros immediately departed the boat according to procedure to avoid casualties and returned fire, destroying the canoe and killing an insurgent. The operation continued for three days. During that time, 10 encampments and three of the local log canoes (or *pirogas*) were destroyed, but no more insurgents were found.[29] While such clear and hold operations are an important part of insurgent destruction, the preparation for them does not go unnoticed, and warning spreads. Consequently, the insurgents generally have adequate time to move, and few of any consequence are captured or killed. Nevertheless, the Bulicoco Archipelago became unsafe to insurgents after October

1962 and remained so until the fuzileiros and launches departed a decade later.

Despite the feverish activity of building the posts and perfecting the naval presence on the Zaire, it took until March 1963 to make the river border effectively secure – virtually a year following the decision to do so. There were a number of factors leading to this delay…

First, the dense growth along the riverbank and the numerous canals – and their even smaller branches – provided the perfect cover for insurgents seeking to infiltrate into Angola.[30] It also took time to learn the river and the likely patterns of effective insurgent evasion. This necessitated the exhausting and inglorious night-patrolling of the canal and river system, the gathering of intelligence and the collective accumulation of knowledge on (and experience with) the Zairian environment and its people.

Second, the LFs and the fuzileiros took time to develop the tactics that worked and to perfect their skill in operating as a team. For instance, such refinements as air reconnaissance were only introduced with the operation in the Bulicoco Archipelago. This resource was indispensable in learning the intricacies of the river and identifying potential enemy trails and encampments.[31]

Third, it took time to gain the confidence of the local population in the wake of the enormous civil disruption and consequent migration. Relations were gradually strengthened, and trust established, but it was slow and patient work. This positive relationship helped with the flow of critical intelligence, as there were few other sources. Tactical

A squad of fuzileiros exploring the canals of Bulicoco Island. (Source: Escola de Fuzileiros)

A fuzileiro patrol monitoring canoe traffic.
Source: Estado-Maior da Armada and *Revista da Armada*)

I say prevented, because there was a confirmation through the intelligence system that pointed to such. But in the obscure world of intelligence and counterintelligence, it is always difficult to know what is true and what is false. However, sometimes we detected signs of this infiltration and immediately conducted sweeps of the area with open demonstrations of force in the inland villages. The incursions were effective, as the population resented its coerced support of the guerrilla, and our action had the effect of scattering the guerrillas. Sometimes they were captured, but later in contact with army forces, others were forced to retreat to their sanctuary in the Congo. Certainly in some cases we were unable to detect their movements, and they found their way into our territory.[32]

Once this power projection was perfected, Portuguese dominance along the Zaire forced the insurgents to move 1,000 kilometers to the east. This was necessary to skirt the naval presence and army patrols in order to reach the internal sanctuary of the Dembos. Neither the posts nor the forces that operated from them were ever challenged in a serious way. Yes, there were the occasional infiltrators moving across the riverine border, but the constant Portuguese naval presence eventually made the land route the preferred one. Mexia Salema quotes a crewmember of the Norwegian cargo vessel *Irma*, which had recently transited the river, as observing that no ship could unload matériel anywhere without being detected by the constant patrols or by the lookout posts.[33] Such security not only safeguarded the fluvial border, but also made the waterway free from insurgent attacks on commercial shipping and military transport.

Experience gained during Operation 'Ferrolho' prompted new thinking on Zairian security. Maintaining seven bases along the 80-mile length was relatively expensive in that it absorbed an inordinate portion of the scarce naval resources available in Angola. Additionally, the enemy could observe a post and note the timing of its patrols. He could then potentially avoid detection and contact. With the introduction of the LDPs into the equation beginning in March 1963, a new concept was born. While the LDPs were designed for moving cargo and personnel, they proved to be enormously versatile in other ways. Beginning with Operation 'Ferrolho', the navy began using the vessels as mobile bases to launch and recover fuzileiros in their rubber boats. The standard LDP was modified to permit 12 to 15 fuzileiros to live on board for short periods by sheltering the hold and outfitting it with bunks, installing refrigerated chests for rations, adding a communications suite and mounting an Oerlinkon 20 mm machine gun for defense.

intelligence and its development thus became the *de facto* duty of the local forces.

Fourth, it took time to establish the logistical support required to maintain the posts and the vessels and men operating from them. The decision to build the posts and their actual construction ran well ahead of the needed support in transport and infrastructure development. It was a patchwork system that improved over time as resources became available in Angola, but in the early stages forced the troops to live and work under harsh and spare conditions, and thus limited their initial capability.

By the spring of 1963, the network was complete and the complementary force of launches and fuzileiros had learned the river system and its land approaches intimately. Each launch operated on average 22 days per month, and missions lasted between three and five days each. This operational tempo produced a constant presence.

Talhadas offers an appraisal of the effectiveness of these patrols based on his experience:

> Apparently our missions of patrolling the margins under our control prevented the infiltration of guerrilla groups.

Fuzileiros conducting a patrol on Bulicoco Island; note the 45-horsepower outboard motors.
(Source: Personal archive of José Augusto Pires de Lima)

LDM 403 converted into a mobile base. The armor plate shield has not yet been installed on the Oerlinkon mount.
(Source: Escola de Fuzileiros)

Also from 1965 onward, the launches were re-gunned by substituting the more modern German-origin MG-42 for the outdated World War Two-vintage von Dreyse light machine gun. For the naval crews, the newer Heckler and Koch G-3 series assault rifle – the standard for fuzileiros – replaced the older Fábrica de Braço de Prata (FBP) m/947 9 mm machine pistol. While the Oerlinkon machine guns remained open mounts, an armor plate shield was added for protection of the gunner.[34]

This new waterborne capability not only added flexibility, mobility and surprise to river operations, but also proved far less expensive to sustain than the system of naval posts. Attacking the problem of river security with an increased intensity and applying the lessons and experiences gathered to date, the team of small landing craft, launches and fuzileiros ranged the length of the Zaire River border, successfully penetrating the canal system and denying it to the enemy. As a consequence, plans were made to consolidate the fixed presence on the Zaire and to deactivate several of the posts following Operation 'Ferrolho'.

Talhadas again shares his experience on the Zaire during this period:

The patrols were conducted in Zodiac boats with 45-horsepower outboard motors, easy to manoeuvre. The patrolling was done at night: we secured the motors, used paddles and drifted in silence, following the riverbank on our side. Sometimes we entered a small swirl, a disturbance of some sort, that took us away from the riverbank, until the current expelled us, and we returned to the quiet of the normal stream, peaceful, sometimes working to avoid contact with the leafy branches that touched the surface. It was a monotonous exercise, silent, exhausting....

In the silence and blackness of night, we murmured in conversation. We sought to be hushed, as dictated by the military seriousness of the moment, but the daily life of silent patrolling overtook our human tendencies, and we felt an atmosphere of nervous anxiety that a prolonged military operation created.

My drifting partner for the length of the river was almost a "Siamese twin," as we lived side-by-side, hour-after-hour, day-after-day. In our almost "silence-phobia" governed by the patrolling discipline and vigilance, we had to talk, softly, whatever the topic. They were the most banal issues, insipid, to try to give some content to the hollowness of life.

Other times, we hid in the bushes of the riverbank and set an ambush for two or three hours in silence. It seemed like a sepulchral silence. You could hear only the call of the birds or the buzzing of the mosquitos. There was never any success in this type of operation. The guerrillas, naturally, avoided the river at our time and place.[35]

By 1966, the enemy had moved eastward, and the river had become relatively quiet. Paulo Lowndes Marques, a junior fuzileiro lieutenant, observed that the patrols were routine: 'There were occasional incidents with clandestine fishermen, but nothing more. The crocodiles were far more dangerous, but they were more afraid of us than we of them'.[36]

Operation 'Mastro do Traquete' ('Foremast') followed, and during this period the posts of Trident, Puelo and Macala were deactivated in March 1967, May 1967 and December 1969 respectively. Operations at Macala – the post midway between Fetish Rock and Noqui – were actually wound down from May 1967 onward, and it acted increasingly as an intermediate support facility upstream of Fetish Rock until its full deactivation 31 months later. Operation 'Mastro de Traquete' was replaced by 'Mastro de Mezena' ('Mizen Mast') in 1968. By the beginning of 1970, only Quissanga and Fetish Rock effectively remained between Santo António do Zaire and Noqui. These were important facilities, as they marked the boundaries of the most difficult section of the river frontier. Because of their position, they were upgraded to replace the retired post capability and to support

Fuzileiros with a captured crocodile.
(Source: Personal archive of José Augusto Pires de Lima)

Fuzileiros posing with their hunting trophy near their post on the Zaire River. (Source: Personal archive of José Augusto Pires de Lima)

LDP mobile base operations.

Life on the spartan posts passed with the rhythm of a micro-society created by the practical autonomy of semi-isolation. Post routines were ordered by the scheduled launching and recovery of the boats that each supported. The monotony of the missions, the sleepless nights on constant alert, the isolation, the meager living conditions on board both the launches and the posts, and the harshness of the climate tried everyone. Despite all of the vicissitudes and difficulties, the sailors and fuzileiros exhibited an enormous courage and patriotism in the execution of their dangerous duties. Indeed, in virtually every case, this shared experience of officers, petty officers, fuzileiros and sailors bound them for life in a fraternity of those who had served on the Zaire.

Leisure time was plentiful, and the men found many constructive pursuits. They read a great deal; Marques notes that he finally read *War and Peace* cover to cover.[37] Fishing was a popular sport, as excellent fish swam in the river, and their catch provided a welcomed enrichment to the normal fare of field rations. Hunting expeditions were also a great favorite, and game was often added to the menu. The occasional hippopotamus and elephant were also found. Overall, life on the river – despite its isolation and danger – was not an extreme hardship. The men fell into a comfortable work routine governed by the social closeness that a small post of this nature brings. The rhythm was broken only by the monthly relief with the new personnel that it brought and contact with the enemy.

The special detachments of fuzileiros were employed both on the river and in the littoral – often in coordination with the army forces at Santo António do Zaire and Noqui – to effect the complementary navy mission of controlling the river approaches. Because of the effective river presence, it meant that the insurgents preferred to cross the land frontier into Angola, an area that was infinitely more difficult to police. They found it easy to cross quietly in places and at times that were free of Portuguese troops. The terrain along the land border was hilly with high grass, thick groves of trees and hardly a settlement or person, with almost all having fled in 1961.

By the mid-1960s, neither the MPLA nor the UPA/FNLA had met with any substantial success in a classic subversion of the population in the north, or in truly displacing the Portuguese position there. This lack of insurgent progress occurred for several reasons, as from the beginning the MPLA had been unwelcome in Léopoldville, and following the June 1963 recognition of GRAE as the *de jure* government of Angola, it moved its headquarters to Brazzaville. Its ability to project itself militarily into Angola became almost completely circumscribed by November, and it looked more and more isolated. In January 1964, at its Conference of Cadres (*Conferência de Quadros*) in Brazzaville, it was decided to begin rebuilding the movement as a serious revolutionary force. Part of this plan involved opening a front in the east of Angola through Zambia. The MPLA had made overtures to Kenneth Kaunda, the first President of Zambia, following its independence from Britain in 1964. It had also befriended Julius Nyerere, the first President of Tanzania, likewise following its independence from Britain in 1962. These relationships were to prove fortuitous. Beginning in 1965, Tanzania and Zambia permitted the transit of Chinese and Soviet weapons and MPLA cadres across their territories to the Angolan border. Because of this access, the MPLA was able to open a major offensive and to conduct an intensive insurgent campaign in the Eastern Angolan districts of Moxico and Cuando Cubango. Preparations were begun accordingly, and by the opening months of 1966, proselytizing of the population in the east was evident. The first armed incursions occurred in April, and the war had now clearly moved to the east of Angola. Portuguese resources were redirected to the east and southeast of the territory in response to the new threat. Fuzileiro operations would become an important component of the Eastern Front, and as we shall see, this dramatic projection of a naval presence inland followed the pattern that was set on the Zaire and that was being set in Mozambique.

(Endnotes)

1.   Douglas L. Wheeler, "The Portuguese Army in Angola," *Modern African Studies* 7 (October 1969), p.430.

2.   Douglas L. Wheeler, "African Elements in Portugal's Armies in Africa (1961–1974)," *Armed Forces and Society* 2 (February 1976), p.237.

3.   Estado-Maior do Exército, *Resenha Histórico-Militar das Campanhas de África, Vol. II, Dispositivo das Nossas Forças Angola* [Historical-Military Report on the African Campaigns, Vol. II, Disposition of Our Angolan Forces] (Lisbon: Estado-Maior do Exército, 1989), pp.63–65.

4.   Willem S. van der Waals, *Portugal's War in Angola 1961–1974* (Rivonia: Ashanti Publishing, 1993), p.64.

5.   Wheeler, "The Portuguese Army in Angola," p.431.

6.   René Pélissier, *La Colonie du Minotaure, Nationalismes et Révoltes en Angola (1926–1961)* [The Colony of the Minotaur, Nationalist Movements and Revolts in Angola (1926–1961)] (Orgeval: Editions Pélissier, 1978), p.658.

7.   Ibid., pp.657–660; van der Waals, pp.58–61.

8.   Leonel Alexandre Gomes Cardoso, "A Acção da Marinha em Angola (1961–64)" [Naval Operations in Angola (1961–64)], *Revista de Marinha* (30 September 1964), p.13. See also Leonel Alexandre Gomes Cardoso, "A Marinha em Angola 1961–64" [The Navy in Angola 1961–64], *Anais do Clube Militar Naval* (April–June 1964), p.265.

9.   José Alberto Lopes Carvalheira, "Acção da Marinha em Águas Interiores (1961–1971)" [Naval Operations in Inland Waters (1961–1971)], in the unpublished collection *Participação da Armada na Defesa das Provincias* [Participation of the Navy in Defense of the Overseas Provinces], photocopied manuscript, 1972, p.6.

10. José Talhadas, *Memórias de um guerreiro colonial* [Memories of a colonial warrior] (Lisbon: Ancora, 2010), p.53.

11. Lopes Carvalheira, "Acção da Marinha em Águas Interiores," p.145.

12. Ibid., pp.150–151.

13. Talhadas, *Memórias de um guerreiro colonial*, p.48.

14. Ibid., pp.37–38.

15. Lopes Carvalheira, "Acção da Marinha em Águas Interiores," p.160.

16. René Pelissier, "Militaires, politicos, e outras mágicos" [Military men, politicians and other magicians], *Análise Social* (December 2002), p.3.

17. José Mexia Salema, *Nem a Pátria Sabe, A Marinha na Guerra em* África *1961–1963* [Not Even the Fatherland Knows, The Navy in the War in Angola] (Lisbon: Edições Culturais da Marinha), p.166.

18. A. de Roboredo (*vice almirante*), "Unidades de Fuzileiros em Angola" [Fuzileiro Units in Angola], commentary (despacho), Lisbon, 16 December 1965, Coloredo Box 224/2093, Arquivo Central da Marinha, Antiga Fabrica Nacional de Cordoaria, Rua da Junqueira, Lisbon.

19. Turíbio Abreu, "Infraestruturas Navais no Ultramar" [Naval Infrastructure in the *Ultramar*], *Anais do Clube Militar Naval* (April–June 1967), pp.427–436.

20. A. Pimentel Saraiva, "Postais do Ultramar: Angola–Postal No. 2" [Postcards from the *Ultramar*: Angola – Postcard ⬜ 2], *Anais do Clube Militar Naval* (April–June 1968), p.310.

21. Talhadas, *Memórias de um guerreiro colonial*, p.54.

22. Lopes Carvalheira, "Acção da Marinha em Águas Interiores', p.22.

23. João Carlos da F. Pereira Bastos, "Dois Anos de Comissão no Zaire" [Two Years of Command on the Zaire], *Anais do Clube Militar Naval* (January–March 1965), p.56.

24. John P. Cann, *Contra-Subversão em* África*, 1961–1974: O Modo Português de Fazer a Guerra* [Counter-Subversion in Africa, 1961–1974: The Portuguese Way of War], 2nd ed., rev. Major General Renato F. Marques Pinto (Lisbon: Prefácio, 2005), p.149.

25. Corpo de Fuzileiros, *Part II: Fuzileiros Especiais*, Unpublished History (Lisbon: Ministério da Marinha, 1987), p.30.

26. Abílio Freire da Cruz Júnior, "Evolução das Infra-estruturas da Armada no Ultramar" [Evolution of Naval Infrastructure in the *Ultramar*], in the unpublished collection *Participação da Armada na Defesa das Províncias Ultramarinas* [Participation of the Navy in the Defense of the Overseas Provinces], photocopied manuscript, 1972, p.13.

27. Pereira Bastos, "Dois Anos de Comissão no Zaire," p.51.

28. Ibid., p.68.

29. Ibid., pp.71–72.

30. Mexia Salema, *Nem a Pátria Sabe*, p.167.

31. Pereira Bastos, "Dois Anos de Comissão no Zaire," p.56.

32. Talhadas, *Memórias de um guerreiro colonial*, p.55.

33. Mexia Salema, *Nem a Pátria Sabe*, p.168.

34. Lopes Carvalheira, "Acção da Marinha em Águas Interiores," p.30.

35. Talhadas, *Memórias de um guerreiro colonial*, p.56.

36. Paulo Lowndes Marques, "Cartas Trocadas" [Anecdotal Letters], *AORN* (December 2000), p.7.

37. Ibid.

CHAPTER 3
THE RIVERS OF GUINÉ

Of the three theaters of fuzileiro operations, Portuguese Guinea (or Guiné, today Guinea-Bissau) was the most complicated and most difficult. It was also the most important theater for the navy, for here its activities were vital not only on the tactical, but also on the strategic level. The reason was quite simple: about 80 percent of all cargo and personnel within the theater moved on the water either by sea, or through the river system. Only about 18 percent moved overland, and a mere 2 percent by air.[1] In the final years of the war, when road travel became difficult, fully 85 percent was waterborne. Water transport was equally as important for the PAIGC, and for this reason the policing of river traffic by the navy and its fuzileiros was as important as its transport role. The force that would prevail in Guiné would be the one that could successfully use the waterways to support its land operations while preventing the other from doing the same.[2] As in Angola, the naval mission was to dominate the sea, coastal and river lines of communication and deny their use to the enemy; support the army and the population with its waterborne transportation capability; and project power ashore.[3] These objectives would be accomplished with the potent combination of launches, landing craft and fuzileiros in an attempt to reduce the PAIGC and cut its men and their supplies that flowed into the country.

A Complicated Theater

Guiné remains a complicated land in which to project force – and consequently, is not easy to secure. First, its climate is unappealing and hostile. The country is tropical and was described by Al Venter in 1973 as a 'grim, torrid stretch of swamp and jungle'.[4] Fuzileiro Corporal José Talhadas, on arriving there by air in October 1967 was disillusioned, for hardly had he put his foot on the ground, then a feeling of discomfort passed through his body: '…[A] blazing heat and oppressive humidity seemed to explode my chest. The perspiration followed me always from my first minutes on the ground'.[5] It is a wet and steaming land under a burning sun. The intense humidity and heat make for an oppressive atmosphere. While there is a dry season that provides some relief from November to May, it is not without discomfort.

As the dry season ends, and the sun reaches its seasonal zenith over Guiné, tropical weather systems develop and are characterized by low-pressure areas and strong ascending warm air currents. These updrafts are fed from the continental air mass over the Sahara and create what is termed locally as the 'east wind'. The population experiences it as a hot, dry air current that comes from the desert to the east, absorbs moisture from the soil and vegetation, and carries a fine dust that affects those with respiratory problems.

The rainy season runs from June to October and ensures a high humidity. It is characterized by frequent monsoons that develop from the disequilibrium between the oceanic and continental air masses. These storms are magnified by the shock of the 'east wind' and are characterized by violent electrical activity with the attendant thunder and lightning, tornados, strong winds reaching 60 knots and heavy rainfall. In the coastal region, annual rainfall averages three meters, and in the interior, 1.25 meters.[6]

Talhadas again observes:

> Additionally, as if to emphasise this disagreeableness, in the first hours the most uncontrolled natural fury, a tornado, hit Bissau with enormous gusts of wind and rain so torrential that the streets were filled with such a volume of water that canoes were able to navigate through them perfectly without grounding. The force of the elements presaged an immeasurably violent war.[7]

It is also a land humming with mosquitoes and many other kinds of insect life. Debilitating tropical diseases abound, and are transmitted by these *petites bêtes*. Again, Talhadas describes it as a place:

> …[W]here flies and mosquitoes teemed and seemed to form dangerous "aerial squadrons" that attacked us, principally at night. Before long we felt their devastating effects, although the mosquito nets managed to limit the damage. The next day, my face and other parts of my body were swollen with bites on all sides. Curses and unspeakable words were more than many on awakening at daybreak.[8]

Venomous snakes thrive in such a habitat. Rapid rates of decay denigrate the quality of front-line medical care. In short, the climate becomes a very important component of Clausewitz's friction of war.

The topography of Guiné is likewise difficult. It can be divided roughly into two distinct geographical areas: the west and the north and east. The most important is the western one, which on a tactical level is characterized by a forbidding and inhospitable stretch of mangrove and swamp forests covering the coastal inlets and deltas of half a dozen rivers. Tidal action floods twice daily, and as the water rises, it fills these estuaries and creates vast tracts of impenetrable swamp.[9] Currents in the rivers during flooding and ebbing can reach seven knots – enough to overwhelm the small engines in the majority of river transport. This tidal action particularly affects navigation in certain areas, such as Gadamael on the upper reaches of the Cacine River, where it is only possible for larger vessels to operate on the four or five days of high tide during a full moon.[10] At low tide, vast expanses of dreary mud flats are exposed and impede the projection of naval power through the river system. Vessels must carefully travel their courses in the center of the channels, for they could easily become grounded and mired in the mud during ebb tide. The low water level would then leave them completely stranded, isolated and vulnerable to insurgent attack.

Further, the thousands of miles of Guinean rivers and tributaries are obscured from the air by mangroves and thick foliage, making clandestine insurgent movement simple and its interdiction a difficult military problem. These rivers are navigable by medium and small craft deep into the country and provide vital lines of communication that cannot be matched by the primitive road system. Indeed, many of the roads during the rainy season become rivers themselves, making passage all but impossible. The coast also has many small islands – the most important of which form the Bijagós Islets. The land rises in the northern and eastern interior areas, where the coastal forests gradually disappear, as the terrain changes into the sub-Saharan savannah plain of grasslands and scattered, scrawny trees. Elevation never exceeds 300 meters.[11]

On the strategic level, the Guinean geography also plays an important role. Officially, Guiné has a land area of 36,125 square kilometers, but this twice-daily inundation covers as much as 22 percent of the country, and reduces the surface area to an estimated 28,000 square kilometers. From this figure an additional 3,200 square kilometers can be deducted for the area periodically flooded by rainwater.[12] Under these considerations, the habitable land mass is about 24,800 square kilometers, or about the size of Switzerland. Its land frontier is about 680 kilometers, of which 300 comprise the northern border with Senegal, and 380 the eastern and southern borders with the Republic of Guiné.[13] Guiné is thus so small that the entire country became essentially a frontier and battle zone, making it extremely difficult to defend.

As if these impediments of climate, terrain and geography were not enough of a challenge, the population represented another obstacle as much for the insurgents as for the Portuguese. In 1960, the population was 525,437 and was concentrated in the western coastal delta with about 100 people per square kilometer.[14] The arid eastern half was virtually empty, with about one person per square kilometer, and it was here that insurgent infiltration occurred with the least opposition. Over 99 percent of the population was black and was fragmented into two primary groupings covering 28 ethno-linguistic groups. Indicative of early exposure to the Portuguese, the coastal population is Christian, or animist. The interior peoples are Muslim, reflecting their contact with the ancient interior trade routes from the Gulf of Guiné through Timbuktu to The Maghreb. There were less than 3,000 whites in Guiné.[15] Historically, it had proved devoid of any reasonable economic potential beyond slavery, so it was never a country of white colonization.

On arriving in Guiné, after October 1967, all fuzileiros undertook an indoctrination to adapt them to the aforementioned conditions and the tactics required to be effective and survive. This training was known as PTO (*Preparação Técnica Operacional*, or Operational Technique Preparation) and administered by the DFE completing its deployment and being relieved.

PTO

Despite the best efforts of the training facilities in the *metrópole*, fuzileiros arriving in Guiné were not attuned to the operating environment and

DFE 7 on parade in Bissau in April 1968 after being relieved by DFE 13 and completing its PTO instruction. (Source: Escola de Fuzileiros)

the tactics of the enemy. From 1966 onward, it became obvious that the experience of outgoing units needed to be shared with the newcomers in the host environment.[16] PTO was thus aimed at sensitizing the relief units and focused entirely on counterinsurgency warfare as it was fought in the operational theater. PTO was also a recognition that fuzileiros familiar with the people, culture and geography of Guiné were indispensable to a successful deployment. It proved extremely valuable and paid great dividends in troop effectiveness.[17]

PTO was conducted in the area of Cumeré for Talhadas and the rest of DFE 12, some five miles upriver from Bissau and on the right bank of the Geba River. Here the fuzileiros – under the instruction of DFE 7 – grew accustomed to moving through 200 to 300 meters of muddy slime at a time, which was overhung with an intricate web of vegetation and inundated by the boggy movement of the water.[18] According to Talhadas, it was painful and extremely exhausting work floundering through dark viscous mud that clung to the body and uniform, filled the boots, and when dried, seemed to entangle and restrict all movement. It was the work of a demon, for it was repeated time and time again over a series of months, until the fuzileiros could do it expertly and quickly. Their lives would depend on such skills.[19]

The PAIGC was not the UPA/FNLA or the MPLA. In fact, in the night, the boom of the PAIGC heavy weapons was perfectly audible from all directions, as well as the return fire of artillery from the army redoubts. The PAIGC was better armed and far more aggressive than the nationalist movements of Angola, observed a veteran who had served a tour in Angola and two in Guiné. Indeed, there was a very different atmosphere in Guiné from that of the old colonial Luanda, and here one saw signs of the enemy and felt his presence. This fact was emphasized by the PTO instructors along with other aspects of the training time and time again.[20]

At the conclusion of its PTO, DFE 12 was mentally and physically prepared. Talhadas describes his feeling at the time as one of elevated determination, a certain preoccupation. Yet, the DFE was billeted with the two other DFEs assigned, and their patrols regularly returned from combat with dead and wounded, and reports of the ferocity of the skirmishes: 'Here the war was different. These 'turras' [terrorists] act with effectiveness and skill. They fight with violence and remarkable discipline. They withdraw without leaving their men behind'.[21] To Talhadas, it was obvious that DFE 12 faced an opponent who would not easily have a change of heart.

Naval Commitment

In 1959, the navy established the Maritime Defense Command of Guiné (*Comando de Defesa Marítima da Guiné*, or CDMG), which was integrated into the Naval Command of Cape Verde and Guiné. Later, on 19 May 1961, it strengthened its hand with the arrival in Bissau of two launches – the *Canópus* (P 364) and the *Bellatrix* (P 363) – and two small landing craft, LDP 101 and 102, which would later be modified and re-designated as LDP 301 and 302 respectively. On 6 June, the launch *Deneb* (P 365) was added to this modest fleet. These vessels and their crews comprised the Patrol Launch Squadron Guiné (*A Esquadrilha de Lanchas de Fiscalização de Guiné*, or ELFG), which was commanded by a junior lieutenant and was the first permanent naval presence in the territory. The squadron commander reported to the commander, CDMG and likewise served as his chief of staff. The first deployment of this new force was to Farim at the head of the Cacheu River and then to Bolama, Buba and Bubaque in the south. At each of these villages, a small naval installation was established to support future operations.[22]

In June 1962, the first Detachment (DFE 2) arrived in Bissau on two military aircraft. Its initial assignment was to guard the naval installations in Bissau and to act as a reserve force, and to this end it began nightly patrols of the harbor in rubber boats that would continue until the conclusion of the conflict. The following month, a combat group or platoon was sent to guard the political prisoners on Galinhas Island and remained there until the spring of 1963. The remaining fuzileiros in Bissau continued to perform sentry duty and to act as a security force on support vessels journeying to such destinations as the small village of Enxudé across the river from Bissau, and to the more distant towns of Buba, Bolama and Cacine. This defensive and static posture of garrison duty was clearly not in keeping with the modern fuzileiro concept envisioned by Roboredo. These men should have been operating along the rivers, making contact with the population and seeking out the enemy.

In October 1962, DFE 7 was also deployed to Guiné and installed in Bolama.[23] During this period, the situation in Guiné progressively deteriorated, as the enemy went over to the offensive and expanded its intense subversive activity in an attempt to isolate the region in the south. This was a coordinated offensive in that the PAIGC simultaneously increased contact over a wide and dispersed area along the northern border with Senegal in order to present an unattractive dilemma to the Portuguese authorities. The PAIGC hoped to divide and weaken the already thin government forces by forcing Portugal to protect all fronts at once.

Finally, on 5 December, the military command reacted and a section of fuzileiros, together with two army companies (one from Bissau and the other from Tite) began a reconnaissance mission in the Cachil swamp forest on the island of Caiar at the southern entrance of the Cobade River just west of Catió. There had been reports of armed enemy in the area hard at work subverting the population. In the waterways that encircled Caiar, three launches and two small landing craft established a patrol to prevent any flight – and on the morning of 6 December, disembarked the forces at various points on the island in a cordon and search operation. After advancing about

eight kilometers inland, a section encountered two women, and this contact resulted in an exchange of fire with nearby insurgents.[24] The operation progressed over difficult terrain and was inconclusive in the final analysis, the insurgents having melted away. It did, however, offer the fuzileiros their first experience in joint operations with the army in Guiné.

Until 1968, the control and use of units of fuzileiros were under the direction of the CDMG. His policy was to maintain a reserve in Bissau and to use these fuzileiros only in specific operations that were always undertaken in coordination with and in support of other naval units. This worked well, as these troops were specially trained to conduct patrols, police the rivers and interdict the enemy in the littorals. These operations can be divided into two types: independent ones that involved patrolling and establishing a presence, and those conducted in force to strike at the enemy. When operating independently, the launches would patrol an assigned river for about 12 days, moving mostly at night, anchoring during the day and coordinating with fuzileiros ashore along the littorals. Intelligence provided by the various intelligence services drove the missions and was coordinated through the naval staff.[25] On the other hand, strike operations would generally be assigned to a fuzileiro detachment with its rubber boats or a launch that put them ashore for a specific mission. Aircraft were used regularly, particularly in the Cumbijã River, to help coordinate such operations and to protect the launches from ambush. Unfortunately the radios were not reliable, and this hampered force coordination and effectiveness. Air operations were also used in the Cacine River, especially to protect a convoy.[26]

When the fuzileiros were assigned to secure a river basin, the routine was to patrol the river daily in rubber boats with the support of a medium landing craft. About every fortnight, there would be a large operation that was invariably conducted at night in order to position for an attack at sunrise. *Comandante* Carlos Gomes noted that in the 13 months of his deployment between 1964 and 1966, he conducted 28 or 29 operations as the Executive Officer of DFE 10.[27] Only rarely were these done in conjunction with other DFEs.

Fuzileiro river patrols would be varied to keep the enemy off-balance, and the favorite tactic was to spend the night hours floating and silently paddling in areas of likely enemy contact. Often the force would divide, some staying with the boats and others going ashore to establish an ambush. If the enemy were present, he would attack as the fuzileiros were landing and at their most vulnerable. When traveling on a launch, the fuzileiros felt exposed, as the launch could be heard a good 10 minutes before its arrival. Also, the rivers were often only 100 meters wide, and the launch was extremely susceptible to RPG fire. Gomes remembers that as Commanding Officer of the launch *Lira* (P 361) between 1971 and 1973, he was attacked eight times by enemy RPGs, and only one hit his vessel.[28] Fortunately the insurgents had very bad aim, even at 50 meters.

Once ashore, the fuzileiros were more adaptive – and walking quietly, could surprise an unsuspecting enemy. They traveled light and carried only five pouches of ammunition clips, a little food and drinkable water. Mobility was the most important factor. They were armed with lightweight aviation rockets (37 mm) launched from an

LFG *Sagitario* (P 1131) on patrol in the Cacheu River, Guiné, 1968 aided by a Dornier observation aircraft.
(Source: Personal archive of Nino Vieira Matias)

Zebro III rubber boats pierside at Ganturé, River Cacheu, Guiné in November 1972 manned by from left to right: Seaman First Class FZE Ribeiro, Corporal FZE Búzio, Second Lieutenant FZE Melo e Sousa and Seaman First Class FZE Carreiras.
(Source: Personal archive of Abel Melo e Sousa)

A *Zebro III* patrol on the River Cacheu in November 1972 shows the vegetal overhang along the riverbank.
(Source: Personal archive of Abel Melo e Sousa)

The standard of DFE 13. All fuzileiro units had their own standard of similar design.
(Source: Escola de Fuzileiros)

LFG *Sagitario* (P 1131) patrolling the Cacheu River, with air support from a Dornier DO-27; note the rocket canister under the wing of the Dornier. (Source: Personal archive of Admiral Nuno Vieira Matias)

LDM 301 landing a section of DFE 13 on a *bolanha* in the Cacheu River. (Source: Personal archive of Admiral Nuno Vieira Matias)

A section of DFE 13 attempting radio contact during a rest stop while conducting an independent operation; the Cacheu River can be seen in the background. (Source: Archive of DFE 13 Veterans)

A section of DFE 13 on independent operations between the Cacheu River and Senegal. The fuzileiros traveled light and moved quietly to achieve mobility and stealth. (Source: Archive of DFE 13 Veterans)

An Alouette III extracting DFE 13 casualties from a combat zone in Guiné. (Source: Archive of DFE 13 Veterans)

Fields of rice cultivation behind a fuzileiro of DFE 13 in the north of Guiné. (Source: Archive of DFE 13 Veterans)

Fuzileiro Corporal Alves (foreground) and 1st Sgt Reis of DFE 1 exploring a canal on the Sambuiá Peninsula in November 1972 in the midst of the rainy season. (Source: Personal archive of Abel Melo e Sousa)

Fuzileiros of DFE 1 being recovered from an operation by an LDM in the midst of the prop roots and branches of mangrove that form a nearly impenetrable web (*taraffe*) along the bank of the Sambuiá Peninsula in November 1972. (Source: Personal archive of Abel Melo e Sousa)

Fuzileiros of DFE 13 burning huts of an enemy base in the north of Guiné. (Source: Archive of DFE 13 Veterans)

Arcturus (P 1151) returned to the Cumbijã River in January 1973; note the refuelling drums for the rubber boats on the deck.
(Source: Personal archive of Abel Melo e Sousa)

Fuzileiros of DFE 8 crossing a dike near Calaque in February of 1973 during a rare break in the rainy season.
(Source: Personal archive of Abel Melo e Sousa)

LFG *Arcturus* (P 1151), LFG *Sagitario* (P 1131) and LFG *Cassiopeia* (P 373) moored at Ganturé patrol base on the right bank of the Cacheu River in 1968. (Source: Personal archive of Admiral Nuno Vieira Matias)

Fuzileiros from DFE 12 crossing a clearing at the edge of dense bush.
(Source: Corps of Fuzileiros)

Fuzileiros from DFE 12 wading across a *bolanha* at the edge of the Cacheu River.
(Source: Corps of Fuzileiros)

operations in the army vision alongside its own Special Forces. The CDMG was forced to bow to army wishes. In February 1967, a directive returned the fuzileiros to CDMG control for naval operations in the Cachu, Cacine and Cumbijã River systems. The launch-fuzileiro teams patrolling these rivers were then able to extend their reach with consequent effectiveness. Control and use changed again with the arrival of General Spínola in 1968 and the implementation of his perceived solutions to immediate security problems. From the strategic view this change was short-sighted, as it broke up an effective launch-fuzileiro team that was denying the use of the rivers to the enemy. In any event, during the final years of the war, squads of fuzileiros were routinely deployed on launches to counter the aggressiveness of the enemy and its ambushes. While this move helped the crews of the launches as a defensive measure, it impeded the fuzileiros in their original mission of continuing the patient and methodical offensive against the enemy logistical system.

Fuzileiros Make Their Mark

On 4 November 1963, the packet boat *India* disembarked DFE 8 in Bissau, a unit that would become one of the most valorous in the Portuguese armed forces under the leadership of *Comandante* Guilherme Alpoim Calvão.[31] Calvão and DFE 8 received their baptism of fire with Operation '*Júpiter*' conducted in the region of Jabadá, where they engaged the enemy twice. Shortly thereafter in Operation '*Trevo*' ('Shamrock'), conducted between 20

adapted tube, three MG-42 machine guns and sometimes a mortar. Gomes remembers slipping past sentries who were smoking and into a village to capture weapons and a potato sack of hand grenades.[29] The enemy would melt away when confronted by the fuzileiros, except in the south of Guiné, where regular PAIGC troops had infiltrated. There were few army positions there, and the navy likewise had less presence in the area. The PAIGC thus was able to develop a strong position in the southern border area and maintain its staying power in the face of weak challenges.

By 1965, this naval-only mission was under some pressure, and its oversight by the CDMG was viewed by the overall theater commander as out of step with what the army saw as the role of Special Forces. The army little understood the naval dimension of the conflict and the use of the fuzileiros in seemingly routine, unspectacular, but vitally important operations against the waterborne logistics network of the enemy.[30] There was a tendency by the army to see fuzileiros as simply another source of specially-trained manpower to undertake

and 29 November, the detachment killed some enemy, captured others and recovered a great deal of diverse war matériel around the village of Darsalame on the left bank of the Cumbijã River and on the Cubisseco Peninsula opposite Como and its sister islands. Two fuzileiros were wounded in the action. While the fuzileiros occupied Darsalame, the commander-in-chief arrived to raise the national flag over the village in an emotional ceremony, as the PAIGC flag had flown there for the preceding eight months.[32]

Como and its adjacent islands were considered important both to the insurgents and to the Portuguese command for obvious reasons. From the point of view of the insurgents it was a perfect staging point, for it was remote, and this isolation brought with it security. It could be supplied by sea from the sanctuary of Guiné only about 25 miles distant or a few hours at most by canoe, and it provided a springboard for PAIGC subversive operations further into Portuguese territory. From the Portuguese point of view, it was perceived as a festering sore of insurgent activity and an unwelcome subversion of its population.

Fuzileiros of DFE 12 waiting for an LDM and re-embarkation at the edge of a *bolanha*; notice the dike system for rice growing. (Source: Corps of Fuzileiros)

Fuzileiros of DFE 2 being loaded into landing craft for Operation *'Lima'* in May 1963 from the frigate *Nuno Tristão* with a destination of Fulacunda. (Source: Central Archive of the Navy)

The insurgents were diverting the local rice crop and livestock to their own ends and establishing themselves as a relatively permanent fixture within the population. Portuguese intelligence estimated the PAIGC force on the three islands to be about 300, which number included about 15 military advisors from Guiné.[33]

Operation *'Tridente'*

During the rainy season of 1963–64, the PAIGC began to use the elevated water levels to cross the Cobade and Cumbijã Rivers and enter the Melo Canal to supply PAIGC forces in the direction of Cacine. The islands of Caiar, Como and Catunco along this route thus became critical in resupplying the area around Catió and the south of Guiné. To this view, it had captured four Portuguese commercial motorboats: the *Mirandela* (March 1963), the *Arouca* (March 1963), the *Bandim* (May 1963) and the *Bissau* (May 1963) for the specific purpose of logistically servicing its military operations. The capture of the first two motorboats prompted Operation *'Sapo'* ('Toad') in March 1963 in which DFE 2 and associated army units conducted security sweeps on the island of São João in the region of Quinara. Later in May, DFE 2 conducted Operation *'Lima'* near Fulacunda, again in the region of Quinara.[34] More needed to be done, however, to destroy the PAIGC logistic system.

For the PAIGC with the newly-acquired motorboats, the normal procedure was to depart Conakry on a periodic basis and navigate northward to the frontier. The vessels remained within the protected coastal territorial waters of the Republic of Guiné and thus by international law were theoretically immune from attack. By the end of 1963, one and possibly two of these PAIGC vessels were further transporting arms and munitions into Portuguese territory, and particularly into the adjoining islands of Como, Caiar and Catunco from the coastal depots of Kadigné and Boké. These three islands were being used to conduct operations and train new recruits. Enemy confidence was such in this area that a Portuguese motorboat was attacked and sunk at the confluence of the Cumbijã and Cobade Rivers on 8 July 1963. The Portuguese ferry *Bor* was attacked on the Cobade River four months later on 19 November, causing the loss of supplies and a casualty.[35] These attacks led to the 1963 and 1964 naval expansion in Guiné. While the Portuguese initiated certain defensive measures, such as modified convoy procedures and upgraded armor and armament on the LFs, the most important actions were the new offensive search and destroy missions of the fuzileiros.

By now, a serious Portuguese challenge was long overdue. The navy in particular worried that without such action, its access to Catió would be closed.[36] Accordingly, a joint operation styled Operation *'Tridente'* would combine army, navy and air force resources to isolate and sanitize the familiar islands of Caiar, Como and Catunco. Como had been the scene of the earlier 8 December 1962 Operation *'Jeta'*, a sweep through the island by DFE 2 with no lasting effect. It was here during contact with the enemy that the first fuzileiro was wounded in combat in Guiné.[37] Now it was the island of Como that again attracted attention.[38]

The three islands comprised the *'Tridente'* area of operations and covered nominally some 210 square kilometers of land, only 170 of which were actually usable because of the tides. All three were characterized by large tracts of rice patties, with their intricate dike systems and alternatively by vast areas of very dense and impenetrable grasslands and swamp forests. These latter areas provided ideal hiding places for insurgents, as troops found passage through them very difficult.[39] *'Tridente'* was anticipated to last for more than two months and from the naval perspective, was supported by a substantial portion of its resources in Guiné.[40]

The naval concept of operations in this effort was, first, to isolate the area by securing the surrounding waterways of the Caiar, Cobade and Cumbijã Rivers; next, to disembark and support the fuzileiros and other land forces in their sweep for enemy troops; and last, to secure the maritime and riverine lines of communication so that a permanent presence could be maintained in the area. The operation was divided into three phases: the first began on 15 January 1964 with the landing of between 1,100 and 1,200 troops in five groups at various sites on the islands:

Landing fuzileiros on Como Island in Operation 'Tridente', January 1964. LDM 101 was later renumbered as LDM 204. (Source: Central Archive of the Navy)

Group A: Cavalry Company 487 and DFE 7

Group B: Cavalry Company 488 and DFE 8

Group C: Cavalry Company 489

Group D: DFE 2

Group E: Infantry Company 577

The landings were given close air support, and artillery provided fires from a support base in Catió some five to 10 miles distant, depending on where one was on the island group. Dorniers and Alouette IIs served as airborne command posts and medical evacuation resources. As one might suspect, there was a challenge to the amphibious assault, and the landings encountered sporadic resistance from the insurgents and their local recruits. The enemy attempted to flee the islands in canoes or on foot, or to hide in the swamp forests. The second phase occurred between 17 and 24 January and was centered in patrolling the three islands to establish a wide presence, to flush out insurgents and to gather intelligence.

During the initial phase, DFE 8 was to establish a beachhead in the south of Como next to Catabão Segundo, an abandoned village, and on 15 January the unit came ashore in two LDPs. The action was rapid, and DFE 8 had moved inland to the village of Cauane by the end of the day.[41] In advancing, the fuzileiros encountered sporadic fire from light arms, but their return fire had kept the enemy at a distance. Near Cauane, DFE 8 joined the northern group and raised the national flag over their camp.

During the evening of 17/18 January, the enemy counterattacked Group B violently, and the engagement lasted a full 70 minutes with no success on either side. The only Portuguese casualty was the light wounding of a cavalry company soldier. For the next two months, the entire war in Guiné centered on these three islands, as Portuguese forces attacked and were counterattacked across them. These operations occurred over very difficult terrain characterized by tall, dense and nearly impenetrable bush. The islands were threaded by small watercourses with their slimy banks and beds. These were not only nasty to cross, but were breeding grounds for mosquitos. The fuzileiros were constantly assaulted by the insects, as well as the heat and humidity. While fighting conditions were extremely trying, at the same time this experience served as a proving ground that pushed the fuzileiros to their limits. Calvão now had a true measure of his

Fuzileiros and sailors loading vehicles onto an LDM following Operation 'Tridente', March 1964. (Source: Central Archive of the Navy)

LDM 203 returning from Operation 'Tridente' in March 1964 with a DFE. (Source: Central Archive of the Navy)

unit's competence and was convinced that his fuzileiros were capable of 'delivering the message to Garcia'.[42]

Following the landing and establishment phases, the third phase lasted from 24 January to 24 March and involved periods of intense fighting throughout Como. The primary fighting occurred in the area of Uncomené and in the Cachil swamp forest on Caiar. Land forces continued to advance and on 7 February reached the village of São Nicolau, an enemy stronghold, where they encountered a heavy machine gun. DFE 8 was able to flank the enemy position without being detected and attack it successfully.[43] As the days passed and the fuzileiros advanced, there was sporadic contact with the enemy. DFE 8 joined with DFE 7 on 27 February in an assault on the Cachil swamp forest. With air support from an F-86 Sabre, Portuguese forces advanced through the area – making contact that was at times heavy.[44] It continued in this way until late March and the conclusion of 'Tridente'. By then, enemy presence on the three islands had been dismantled, the prestige of the PAIGC and its leaders reduced, and their confidence destroyed. The respect for Portuguese authority was evident in the population. During 'Tridente', Calvão had organized a nucleus of Guinean guides who endured the same fighting conditions as those of the fuzileiros.[45] Later these guides would serve as the basis for the African DFEs. DFE 8 returned to Bissau on 22 March, as its part in 'Tridente' ended.[46]

The insurgents had suffered substantial losses in 76 killed, 15 wounded and nine taken prisoner – a casualty rate of around 30 percent.[47] These numbers do not, however, consider unknown

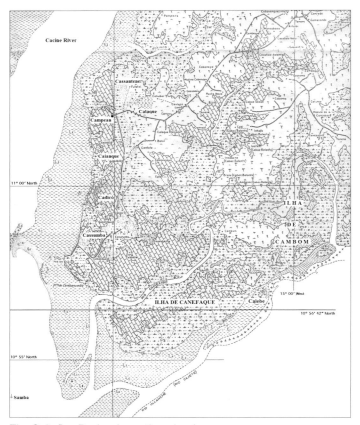

The Quitafine Peninsula southern border area.
(Source: Map drawn by the author)

casualties from artillery fire and close air support. Captured correspondence between PAIGC leaders confirmed their besieged and desperate state and the need for reinforcements.[48] The Portuguese forces suffered nine killed and 47 wounded in the 71-day operation.[49]

The numbers of both local inhabitants and insurgents remained small in the Como Island region, as it subsequently lost its importance to the latter as an area of local support and a refuge in their operations. Calvão confirmed this when he returned to Como five years later in Operation 'Torpedo' with DFE 7 and found only weak resistance.[50] The PAIGC moved progressively northward onto the peninsulas of Quitafine and Cantanhez adjacent to the Guiné border and proceeded to isolate the local market towns of Catió and Bedanda.[51] The ports of these besieged towns, however, remained the secure link to Bissau via the waterways. These moves positioned the PAIGC advantageously to subvert the interior of Guiné, as its lines of communication from its Guinean sanctuary through these two peninsulas became increasingly safe from Portuguese interdiction.

On returning to Bissau, the fuzileiros unwound in various ways. Some ate oysters and drank Cristal beer in the café Zé da Amura, while others recomposed their combat rations with a chicken from a local restaurant, and still others enjoyed entertainment at the nightclub Chat Noire. These experiences broke the monotony of day-to-day life. In other instances, Calvão and his friends would sing opera, play the piano and otherwise enjoy amusing others with their musical skills.[52]

Above: Fuzileiros awaiting the launch of an operation. The fuzileiro to the right is reading a navigation chart; the fuzileiro to his front is killing a mosquito, while the one above is scratching a bite on his leg. Mosquitos were clearly a constant pest. LDM 302 is alongside, with its armored pilot house visible; note the armored porthole shutters that enable the crewmen to protect themselves in a firefight. (Source: Personal archive of José Manuel Malhão Pereira)

Right: LDM 305 with a superior view of its covered hold. Living and messing facilities for the fuzileiros were below and enabled extended fuzileiro operations.
(Source: Personal archive of José Manuel Malhão Pereira)

LDM 201 pierside with LFG Orion (P 362); note the covered hold with the rubber boats lashed atop it. Because of the low water, the deeper draft LFG is outboard of the LDM.
(Source: Personal archive of José Manuel Malhão Pereira)

Two LDMs at Ganturé, with one with its ramp lowered to reveal the fuzileiro cargo bay living quarters afloat; note the fuzileiro detachment standard flying on the launch to the far left.
(Source: Archive of DFE 13 Veterans)

LDM 302, with its Zebro boats astern; note the Oerlinkon 20 mm Mk II gun mount immediately in front of the pilot house and the drum of fuel for the *Zebro* outboard motors on the port side of the pilot house. This LDM likewise features a covered hold.
(Source: Personal archive of José Manuel Malhão Pereira)

LDM 302 during its recovery after a firefight on the Cacheu River. It holds the distinction of having been sunk three times and raised each time to resume duties – a testimony to its durability.
(Source: Escola de Fuzileiros)

Relaxing at the officers' mess at Ganturé in November 1972. From left to right: army doctor, 1st Lt Meireles de Amorim, 2nd Lt Lauret, 1st Lt Pereira Vale, Capt Simões, 2nd Lt Melo e Sousa, 2nd Lt Vicente Cabral, army officer, army officer and 2nd Lt Elias da Costa.
(Source: Personal archive of Abel Melo e Sousa)

Elements of DFE 8 on the deck of an LDM on their way to an operation in 1965.
(Source: Personal archive of José Manuel Malhão Pereira)

1965 Operations

Fuzileiro detachments continued to be used as intervention forces and were sent on either independent or joint operations based on credible intelligence. In February, DFE 8 returned to the Cacheu River in the north with two of its sections, and these patrolled the river on board the *Lira* for two months. In April, the detachment coordinated with Cavalry Battalion 490 in Farim to assault the enemy's Sambuiá base on the frontier with Senegal in Operation 'Mongua'.[53] The raid demonstrated that a section or two of fuzileiros, with their agility and maneuver capabilities, was vastly more lethal than a superior insurgent force, and 'Mongua' showed clearly that the fuzileiros were skilled in leveraging a knowledge of the terrain and its conformation to confound the enemy.[54] The raid damaged the PAIGC, but not enough, as it retaliated with an attack on the *Orion*, now on patrol in the Cacheu. The ambush occurred opposite Porto de Côco, and the vessel was hit 30 times with machine gun fire and twice with RPGs, all of which fortunately did little damage. The ship returned fire with its Bofors 40 mm cannon, and with the fierceness of this action, it was now clear that the war had spread to the north. DFE 8 remained in this sector until the end of its deployment in October and spent a good part of the spring on the *Nuno Tristão* because of the rainy season. The consequent flooded land made operations ashore all but impossible. The shelter of the ship was small comfort, as its interior was impossibly hot and humid. The fuzileiros preferred to be outside whenever the rain lifted.[55]

While the conduct of reconnaissance and armed patrols on the littorals and adjacent terrain to deny them to the enemy was important, it was not the only mission – and not even the most important. The principal one was the maintenance of freedom of navigation for Portuguese forces and its denial to the enemy. For this the fuzileiros set ambushes from their rubber boats throughout the rivers and were enabled in this by the help of the larger launches that carried them to the proximity of the ambush or patrol area. Often when they came aboard naval vessels for any period to conduct these operations, they integrated themselves as much as possible into the ship's company and performed such tasks as manning the forward 40 mm gun mount. They developed a tradition of comraderie that linked them to the naval crews that transported them, launched their rubber boats and landed them ashore. This was important, as both shared the difficult conditions of the campaign, lived together in danger and depended on each other.[56]

After Operation 'Fitaum' in August 1965, it was concluded that the population – now fully behind the enemy politically, militarily and psychologically – would have to be either converted or destroyed; both an impossibility.[57] In fact, the fuzileiros in their actions were systematically destroying canoes, *moranças* (native Guinean huts), cattle, culture and the local way of life. The native population was pressed from both sides and became the loser in the fight. When the fuzileiros entered the bush, the population as a general rule was suspicious and took refuge in the mangroves. It thus fell on the navy and more particularly the fuzileiros, who were in frequent contact with the people, to publish the Portuguese message. The procedure was for the fuzileiros to question the people to determine if they

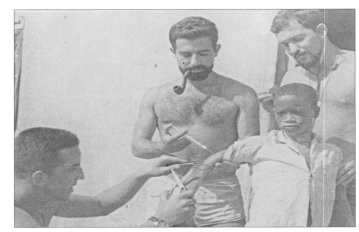

A navy doctor aided by two corpsmen examines and inoculates a Guinean boy. (Source: Archive of DFE 13 Veterans)

The *Ariete* (LDG 102) on a resupply mission in the south of Guiné. (Source: Central Archive of the Navy)

were paying taxes to the PAIGC or aiding the insurgents with food, recruits, shelter and intelligence. If they were doing any of these things, then they were probably subverted, unless participation was clearly against their will.[58] While they might politely listen to the Portuguese message, they remained the hapless victims of the conflict, tethered to the land where they lived and thus unwillingly caught between the two combatants. Nevertheless, the navy and its fuzileiros aided the population in many ways – the most popular being medical support.

The fuzileiros patrolled the Geba and Corubal Rivers permanently now, and this provided some security. In the south, however, the enemy was firmly entrenched along the Cumbijã, and constant operations in this area now required the strength of two or even three DFEs to counter strong, determined resistance from numerous aggressive PAIGC groups.

DFE 8 performed the last mission of its deployment at the end of September when it was sent on Operation 'Fecho' ('Lock') to destroy an enemy encampment in the region of Bricama just to the east of Farim and south of the Jubembem River (an extension of the Cacheu). The detachment split into two assault groups and maneuvered masterfully to inflict heavy losses on the enemy. Overall statistics for this unit for its entire deployment were impressive: it conducted 47 operations (one of which, 'Tridente', lasted 66 days) and experienced 92 firefights. It inflicted 146 enemy deaths, took 38 prisoners, destroyed 89 enemy canoes, burnt 1,600 enemy houses and captured four dozen arms and thousands of rounds of ammunition. It suffered four deaths and 31 wounded.[59]

On 3 October, the first of three large landing craft arrived in Guiné: the *Alfange* (LDG 101). While this addition brought new capability, the enemy was likewise making changes. As he gained experience, his tactics shifted and he began to attack the fuzileiros when they were the most vulnerable during their re-embarking phase, or when infrequent air support had departed the area.[60] In the first instance, the fuzileiros were busy loading themselves into the landing craft or patrol launch and not fully prepared for the enemy to appear. In the second, the enemy lived in fear of aircraft and their capabilities, for he could take only passive defense measures against them until very late in the war. Once he knew he was safe from airpower, he felt free to appear from hiding.

1966 and 1967 – PAIGC Ascendant

By the beginning of 1966, the Cantanhez Peninsula had become a permanent sanctuary in which the PAIGC dominated the landscape. This was evident in the July 1965 failed intervention of three DFEs and again on 21 December, when the three new DFEs supported by a mortar platoon from CF 7 were unable to enter the village of Cafine. The mission was not successful, for the enemy had a well-organized defense, well-trained troops and an abundance of arms and munitions. He was well led; his

Fuzileiros exploring a canal off the Cacheu River in 1965.
(Source: Central Archive of the Navy)

morale was high; and he enjoyed vastly superior numbers. He used the terrain to his advantage and never presented an easy target.[61] The enemy had developed a tactical radio jamming capability and with its radio intercepts and electronic disruption, the fuzileiros lost surprise and the enemy was able to anticipate their movements.[62]

Throughout the remainder of the year, the PAIGC attempted to penetrate the Cacheu barrier in the north, but the strong presence of Portuguese forces along the axis of Binar–Bula–Có–Pelundo–Teixeira Pinto blocked him. As the year advanced, the PAIGC established a string of bases in Senegal opposite the Guinean villages of Susana, São Domingos, Sedengal, Ingoré and Barro – its most significant being Campeda opposite São Domingos. The local population was unhappy about this development and resisted the new PAIGC presence and subjugation.[63] With such a preponderance of force in Senegal putting pressure on Portuguese forces, it was only a question of time before the Cacheu barrier was breached.

As far as the fuzileiros went, the nature of the river system with its tributaries allowed them to penetrate up to 20 kilometers inland from the main body in their rubber boats. Because they were a small, but well trained and experienced force, they were best employed on missions that would likely encounter enemy forces. These would be raids, ambushes and similar strikes, for as light infantry, the fuzileiro staying power was limited. The size of the force applied against the enemy depended on its anticipated size. To ensure success, most fuzileiro operations from mid-1966 consisted of two DFEs operating against a target from different quarters to force the enemy to address multiple threats from different axes. For the remainder of the year, the fuzileiros operated south of the Geba River, where the enemy followed Mao's formula: when the enemy advances, we retreat; when the enemy camps, we harass; when the enemy tires, we attack; when the enemy

Fuzileiros from DFE 13 aboard LFG *Sagitario* (P 1131) in the Cacheu River prepare for an operation in 1968.
(Source: Personal archive of Admiral Nuno Vieira Matias)

Prime Minister António de Salazar awarding *Comandante* Alpoim Calvão the Gold Military Medal for Military Valor with Palm in the Terreiro do Paço; Lisbon, 10 June 1966.
(Source: Central Archive of the Navy)

retreats, we pursue.[64] As before, the greatest danger to the fuzileiros occurred during the vulnerable landing and disembarking with landing craft, or returning and loading into rubber boats. An attack with the launch ramp of a landing craft down could send an RPG into its cargo bay and cause many casualties.

From the PAIGC bases in Senegal, the enemy was finally able to cross the northern frontier and the Cacheu River and spread his influence over a large area, particularly in the vast and difficult Oió forest. His primary conduit for expanded presence now became the Sambuiá Peninsula, and it quickly became known as the 'Sambuiá Corridor' for good reason:[65] the terrain on the Sambuiá is flat, and the surrounding brackish waters are influenced by tidal action that causes the water level to rise and fall several meters. The unproductive land between the high and low tides is without vegetation and is called the *bolanha*. It is filled with hydraulic works that enable the capture and retention of the rains in a vast dike system for growing rice. It is also covered with fishing nets and dense mangrove swamps, so when the fuzileiros disembarked and came ashore from their boats, they were faced with a difficult walk to reach dry land and the forest. When walking through forest, each fuzileiro maintained visual contact with the one in front so as not to become lost. There were often clearings with marshy ground – and often walking through what appeared to be standing water was indeed soft ground that sucked at the fuzileiros' feet and produced a great sense of fatigue.[66] The terrain and climate were as much an obstacle as the PAIGC and caused great friction in every operation.

1968 and 1969: Years of Change

At the time of Spínola's arrival in May 1968, the enemy had expanded his assault on Guiné to encompass the entire land frontier and was making incursions from both the north and east in addition to the south. These borders were largely uncontrolled and open, and incursions were now being made virtually unchecked from the north. The PAIGC cadres crossed the Senegalese border and proceeded along a number of established routes that led to the Cacheu River, across it and into the Oió forest – an internal sanctuary north-east of Bissau. Spínola thus turned his attention toward these avenues of infiltration in a new counter-penetration strategy and directed a number of actions aimed at destroying the four key routes leading from Senegal. Each of these was based on a river crossing, or *cambança*: Sitatô, Jubembem, Sambuía and Canja. Two were named for villages located on the Cacheu River at the crossings, and two others for a small tributary defining the crossing. These corridors were supported by bases located in Senegal: Sincha (Sitatô), Hernacono (Jubembem) and Cumbamory (Sambuía and Canja). Spínola sought to destroy these northern supply corridors

A view along the central 'street' of the former commodity trading center of Gouveia towards the pier of the now Ganturé patrol base. The former warehouses and administrative buildings were in part converted to fuzileiro use. (Source: Archive of DFE 13 Veterans)

The interior of the main warehouse at Ganturé converted to fuzileiro barracks. (Source: Archive of DFE 13 Veterans)

as part of his counter-penetration strategy and force the enemy cadres within Guiné to wither in isolation. His concept was that even though the insurgents may swim among the population like the fish in the sea, they still needed to infiltrate all of the necessities of war such as food, munitions and new troops fresh from the training camps. He would seek to destroy the infiltration routes for these and starve the PAIGC within Guiné, and would do so by launching a series of ambitious and persistent operations against the enemy.[67] He likewise sought to shape a force for its execution, and at the tactical level, this came in the form of the Permanent Operational Commands (*Comando Operacional Permanente*, or COP) and the Permanent Operational Group Commands (*Comando de Agrupamento Operacional Permanente*, or CAOP) to which he assigned the detachments of special fuzileiros.

During the spring of 1968, a number of operations were conducted in the north whose purpose was to locate and destroy the enemy logistic capability along a 12-kilometer front between the mouths of the Dunor and Quissir Rivers: two small tributaries of the Cacheu that straddle the Canja Corridor. This would begin to deny the key established passages to PAIGC forces for moving their war matériel

into the territory – and in May and June, DFEs 3, 10, 12 and 13 (which were now assigned to Guiné) began their operations on the Cacheu; their initial engagements, Operations 'Alnair' (variously 'Al Na'ir' – May 1968) and 'Aldebaran' (June 1968) were launched from mobile bases aboard the launches and were a great success. As a result, the Canja Corridor was effectively shut, and a frustrated enemy was forced to seek other routes or to see his operations wither.

This success encouraged Spínola to expand the operation, and he now sought to increase the Cacheu blockade to 60 kilometers. This ambitious plan required an expanded support infrastructure to accommodate a significantly augmented force, and a needed naval base was established at Ganturé on the right bank of the Cacheu just south of Bigene. This Patrol Base Ganturé (*Base de Patrulhas de Ganturé*, or Bapat de Ganturé) became the headquarters of Permanent Operational Command Three (COP 3).[68]

When the fuzileiros arrived at Ganturé, they found an old colonial warehouse, three dilapidated sheds and a small dock that had once been the home of a branch of the concession company António Silva Gouveia, which had overseen the export of peanuts (*mancarra*)

Fuzileiros reinforcing one of the six bunkers at Ganturé with concrete-filled drums as additional protection against RPG attacks. (Source: Archive of DFE 13 Veterans)

and cacheus.[69] The primary warehouse, known as 'Casa Gouveia', was repaired. The sheds, however, were removed and new base infrastructure was put in place over the next several months. One feature consisted of a series of six small concrete shelters about 10 x 3 meters, literally bunkers, which were able to offer protection to the fuzileiros from mortar and RPG attacks.[70] These were arranged in a semi-circle, three on each side of a sort of central 'street' that was little more than a track cut from the bush. It led from a quay of wood and concrete-filled drums on the Cacheu in a virtual straight line north toward Bigene, a village some three kilometers distant. Here there was an army company and a heavy artillery platoon with three British 5.5 in howitzers, known to the Portuguese as 'Obus 14s'. Bapat de Ganturé, and its complement of two DFEs and a platoon of naval fuzileiros, was enclosed entirely by a barbed wire perimeter.[71] With a new base and a new strategy for destroying the enemy lines of communication, Bigene and Ganturé assumed a heightened role at the center of an area that extended from Barro in the west to Guidaje in the east on the right bank of the Cacheu, and from Brufa in the west to Tancoroal in the east on the left bank.

The daily operational routine outside of the larger, planned operations consisted of establishing a presence on the river and its littorals through water and land patrols. The patrolling section of 10 to 15 men was apportioned in up to four rubber boats, with three to four men in each. They carried the usual light weapons: a bazooka, an MG42 machine gun and G3 rifles equipped with grenade launchers. Among them was a radioman with a TR28 transceiver to communicate with Ganturé and a PRC216 radio to talk between boats. The typical water patrol lasted a week in a targeted area, and put the men on call 24 hours a day. After returning from it, the fuzilerios would have a short rest before rotating to land operations.[72] River and land operations were alternated for a section as much as possible to provide variation.

Talhadas describes water operations as a 'small village of fuzileiros'

moving continuously along the banks of the Cacheu and its tributaries on elevated alert. The patrols were aimed at areas of high enemy traffic – a situation that exhausted the fuzileiros with its necessary concentration and restiveness. The patrol sought the hidden creeks and canals that served as sites to ambush the enemy, and as terminals for the enemy canoes that crisscrossed the Cacheu with men and supplies. As the fuzileiros established themselves on the river, it became clear that the enemy followed the progress of the boats and selectively attacked them when the opportunity arose. Sometimes the fuzileiros were injured or killed, and at other times the insurgents became successful targets before they could disappear into the matted mangrove growth.[73]

In June, Operations 'Via Láctea' ('Milky Way') and 'Andrômeda' were initiated to extend the success of Canja, increase security on the Cacheu and foreclose the other enemy transit corridors. The number of forces participating was expanded with additional army units, and land operations around Olossato, Bigene, Binta, Farim and Porto Coco sought to reduce the PAIGC assault. By September 1968, enemy presence on the Sambuiá Peninsula had increased and hardened, and the PAIGC continued to dominate the river crossings there. The two operations ran into December, but by then Spínola was beginning to gain control of the river and its approaches.[74]

Following 'Via Láctea' and 'Andrômeda' in December, DFEs 12 and 13 in Operation 'Dragão 68' ('Dragon 68') had surprised the enemy in this area, defeated him, captured diverse war matériel and taken into custody a number of civilians. In the course of the operation, the fuzileiros had encountered large numbers of the population who were friendly and supportive of the Portuguese and who had told them of the many PAIGC arms caches on the peninsula. This intelligence laid the groundwork for immediate future operations.

In January 1969, as a follow-up on this intelligence, Operation 'Grande Colheita' ('Great Harvest') was planned – and as it unfolded, the participating army troops discovered a number of the caches, recovered seven or eight arms and some munitions, and called the air force to destroy the remainder with napalm attacks. The on-scene army commander sent a message to Spínola apprising him of the discovery and intended destruction. Spínola immediately summoned a helicopter and shortly arrived on the Sambuiá Peninsula. On appraising the situation, he concluded that paratroops should be brought from Bissau and inserted by helicopter to complete the search for additional caches. Lieutenant Nuno Vieira Matias, the commander of DFE 13, reminded Spínola that the fuzileiros were trained and

Fuzileiros negotiating an area of matted mangrove growth. (Source: Escola de Fuzileiros)

Recovering fuzileiros near Cachamba Papel, Tombali Peninsula, in the south of Guiné; February 1973. (Source: Personal archive of Abel Melo e Sousa)

and Soviet pornographic magazines.[75]

By the end of the day, Spínola decided that the fuzileiros should stay in the immediate area to be positioned for operations the following day. The fuzileiros, however, had concerns about this decision, as they were being asked to remain overnight without food or water, within a few short kilometers of the Senegalese Frontier and under conditions that would be extremely dangerous after dark. While there would be fire support from the artillery platoon in Bigene that could cover a two-mile radius of the fuzileiro encampment, for the fuzileiros there was considerable question as to what the accuracy of the battery might be. Matias told the pilot of the last departing helicopter to relay

experienced in helicopter insertions and were immediately available. Spínola agreed and gave the order. It was thus that 40 fuzileiros from DFE 13 began the search, forgoing their packs and even drinking water so that the five assigned Alouette III helicopters could carry the maximum weight in captured arms and munitions. Soon an enormous cache of matériel was discovered. Close air support was provided, as the site was near the frontier, and there was thus a strong threat of a counterattack from Cumbamory. The helicopters began the evacuation of the arms and worked all day, as the discovery included over 100,000 munitions, about 200 light and heavy weapons, uniforms, medicines, educational material and moreover, perfume

to Spínola that the fuzileiros would be at a place in the forest marked on the pilot's map where there would be large trees and where they would be able to protect themselves during the night, if detected by personnel coming from Senegal.[76]

At the end of the afternoon, with the departure of air support, the fuzileiros began to be bombarded with mortar fire and felt that darkness could not come soon enough. When it finally did arrive, they moved away under a well-practiced procedure of silently abandoning a position and leaving the enemy wondering where they had gone. It was fortunate they followed this plan, as during the night, people came to the site. The next day, the fuzileiros completed the removal of

A section of African fuzileiros posing on the stern of an LFG in the harbor of Bissau in November 1971.
(Source: The Michael Calvert Collection, Liddell Hart Centre for Military Archives, King's College London)

Corporal José Talhadas receiving the Medal of Military Valor with Palm from General Spínola on 10 June 1971 in the courtyard of the Governor's Palace. Afterward, both spoke in conversation during refreshments in the garden of Fort Amura.
(Source: Personal archive of José Talhadas)

the matériel and fought an engagement to the north of the peninsula, where they captured 11 Czechoslovakian M25 submachine guns.[77] At the end of the second day and into the evening, the only available drinking water came from the pools of rainwater along the *bolanha* – not a particularly healthy option. With the conclusion of '*Grande Colheita*', DFE 13 held the record for the largest discovery of war matériel by a single unit in a single operation. This represented a heavy blow to the PAIGC and a welcomed decrease in pressure on Portuguese troops in the north of Guiné.[78]

While these operations were aggressive and successful in disrupting PAIGC incursions, they were defensive in nature. The PAIGC threat remained alive in its sanctuaries of Senegal and Guiné, and Portuguese thoughts of offensive cross-border operations became a tempting consideration. While such operations were well within the Portuguese capabilities, they would entail a new dimension of political risk that could bring unforeseen difficulties.

African Fuzileiros

On 21 April 1970, as part of Spínola's policy of Africanizing his force that was always short of manpower, the navy commissioned its first detachment of African fuzileiros: DFE 21. Candidates for this first of what was to be three DFEs were selected from 900 volunteers. Such overwhelming popularity was easily understandable, as a DFE was considered the ultimate elite unit. The 150 men chosen came from those already serving in the armed forces in some capacity as militiamen, sailors, or those otherwise familiar with naval life. As always in Africa, consideration needed to be given to a candidate's origin and ethnicity – a factor whose omission initially created problems in the formation of DFE 21, but was corrected with DFEs 22 and 23.[79] The training center for the African fuzileiros was established in Bolama and consisted of barracks, classrooms, messing facilities, a parade and so on. Instruction was administered by the School of Fuzileiros, and instructors came from the Vale do Zebro to conduct an accelerated and improvised course. On graduation of the first class of special fuzileiros, DFE 21 was formed with Lieutenant Raul Eugénio Dias da Cunha e Silva as its Commanding Officer.[80] DFE 22 followed on 16 November 1971 and DFE 23 on 1 July 1974.

Road to 'Mar Verde'

In the south of Guiné, the four PAIGC supply bases across the frontier had played a pivotal role in the infiltration. These bases were supported from Conakry by an assortment of the locally-manufactured motor launches *Arouca*, *Bandim*, *Bissau* and *Mirandela*. The PAIGC could now project power from Conakry to the depot of Kadigné on the island of Tristão and then to the Portuguese islands of Canefaque and Cambon.[81] From these islands, a large fleet of canoes and modest numbers of small outboard motor boats consistently penetrated the waterways of Southern Guiné largely unchallenged and effectively extended the PAIGC distribution system and consequent combat capability well into the interior. The south of Guiné was, as a consequence, thoroughly infiltrated by the PAIGC by 1969, and this dominance posed a most serious threat to Spínola's plans. Coincident with this development was the reassignment of Calvão as the Chief of the Special Operations Department of the Commander-in-Chief. The first step was Spínola's authorization of two significant operations to contest and disrupt the intense PAIGC traffic: Operation *'Nebulosa'* ('Nebulous') and Operation *'Gata Brava'* ('Wildcat').

It must be said that following the move away from operations along the Camexibó, Nhafuane and Inxanche Rivers in June 1964 because of the fear of offending Sékou Touré, the PAIGC had moved quickly and steadily to fill the vacuum. The consequent result was that Portuguese land forces were increasingly facing a well-armed and supplied PAIGC. The volume of supplies and troops moving into Guiné virtually unchallenged created a difficult and obvious problem.

'Nebulosa' was conducted between 15 and 27 August 1969 and was intended to intercept and destroy the PAIGC boats and any other enemy craft and their crews in the waters of the Inxanche River, which marked the frontier with Guiné. In preparation for this mission, Calvão began to form an intelligence picture aided by an older sailor named Abou Camará, who was held in detention and had served on PAIGC vessels, including the *Patrice Lumumba*, of which we shall hear more in a minute.[82] Following some encouragement and an offer of amnesty, the prisoner became cooperative and decided to collaborate completely. He revealed that the PAIGC transit of the Inxanche was always conducted at high tide, that all of the boats in Kadigné worked for the PAIGC and that all of the transiting enemy boats needed to use and violate Portuguese territorial waters.[83] Given these facts, Calvão developed a concept of operations in which he would lay an ambush using fuzileiros in rubber boats hidden along the Portuguese shore.

In the first days of August, the LFG *Sagitário* (P 1131), whose commanding officer would act as the overall commander of *'Nebulosa'*, conducted a night reconnaissance of the anticipated area of operations.[84]

He took *Sagitário* to the vicinity and launched a rubber boat with fuzileiros to explore the Inxanche riverbank. The small force made good use of the darkness, low tide and frequent rain showers as cover for a successful and undetected reconnaissance. The conclusion was that the small mangrove island of Calebe was the ideal ambush site.

Finally, on 24 August at 2300, Calvão returned – and with his section of fuzileiros in four rubber boats. The small force reached its destination of Calebe by 0300 on 25 August completely undetected.[85] When the boats reached the island, which was covered with thick foliage and a confusing entanglement of mangrove trees and their tough prop roots, the fuzileiros used a saw and machete to cut an opening through them and gain access to a narrow canal that would be their home for more than 54 hours. After backing the boats into the canal with their bows out, the entrance was camouflaged and closed with mangrove branches. The canal was so shallow that at low tide the boats could be completely grounded, particularly if the sea height was below normal. This was not anticipated to be a problem, as intelligence indicated the large PAIGC vessels came into the river only at high tide. As time passed, the strong rain showers peculiar to the area resolved the drinking water problem and served to cover the noise of the outboard motors, all of which were tested routinely. During the rain the motors had to be covered, as the high humidity tended to make them unreliable. After the rain came the mosquitoes.[86] During the waiting period, the fuzileiros observed an intense amount of canoe traffic between the two sides of the river, principally at night. Indeed, the ambush cover was often brushed by these transiting craft, and their occupants felt wholly at home and chatted freely, oblivious to any danger. During the long and boring wait on 26 August, the fuzileiros heard a motor boat from Kadigné pass very close in the dark, but were not permitted to assault it amid great disappointment and much cursing.[87]

On 27 August towards 0930 as the sea was beginning to ebb, the fuzileiros heard the muffled noise of a motor to the left of their position. All prepared for action – and as soon as the vessel was identified as being manned by the PAIGC and being in Portuguese territorial waters – the motors on the rubber boats were started for an attempted ambush. The interception began with a stern chase, as the long immobilization of the motors caused some to operate unevenly. Calvão's boat took the lead and pulled abreast of the target, a vessel that sailed without a flag or other identification. When the fuzileiros signalled for it to stop, it increased speed and veered toward the entrance canal to Kadigné. Calvão's boat accelerated and drew to within five meters of the target, at which point he called in French and ordered it to stop. The response was some light arms fire, which was returned with a fusillade from the fuzileiros.[88]

Calvão's boat closed the gap, and the sailor Tristão flung himself at the vessel, scrambled aboard and entered the lower deck, followed by his translator, Abou Camará.[89] Meanwhile, Calvão boarded the upper deck and engaged in some hand-to-hand combat that was rapidly concluded with the arrival of the other three boats and their fuzileiros. In the midst of the fray, a canister of tear gas was loosed; the helmsman of the vessel became incapacitated and it went out of control. With its throttle wide open, it ran aground in the heavy growth lining the south bank of the river, and three or four men were tossed into the water. Petty Officer André gained control of the helm, and Petty Officer Abrantes Pinto, an experienced motorman mechanic, had no trouble with the engine. Between these two they refloated the vessel and set a course for the mouth of the Inxanche, all the while weeping from the effects of the gas.[90]

The vessel was identified as the *Patrice Lumumba* and carried 24 persons, who were made prisoners. It was also carrying several tons of provisions and a supply of weapons, mainly light arms. Among the passengers were three PAIGC officials, one of whom was section secretary for Kafarande. Unfortunately, he had been killed in the skirmish.

The vessel proceeded with fuzileiro escort to a rendezvous with *Sagitário*, which attempted to take it in tow for a return to Bissau. Things did not go well, and despite the best efforts of the crew, the *Patrice Lumumba* was too damaged from its collision with the formidable mangroves and the exchange of fire to continue afloat. It sank in 12 meters of water while being towed across the mouth of the Cacine River.

It was some months before another such operation was mounted, as the PAIGC initially seemed to take a more cautious profile on the Inxanche following the loss of the *Patrice Lumumba*. Nevertheless, the insurgents soon recovered and moved again into the security vacuum left with the completion of *Nebulosa* and the lack of any continuous naval presence on the Inxanche to challenge them. The navy was to return on 6 March 1970, some seven months later, with Operation 'Gata Brava'. In the meantime, enemy logistic operations expanded dangerously, with adverse consequences for Spínola's campaign…

In the first days of February 1970, Spínola's staff received information that a PAIGC launch, likely the *Bandim*, would be bringing an enemy element from Boké to Kadigné on or about the 25th of the month. Calvão was given responsibility for planning an interception of the vessel and the capture of its personnel. Accordingly, he established an ambush with a team of eight fuzileiros in two rubber boats at the entrance of the canal leading to Kadigné over the evening of the 24th and the dawn of the 25th. Unfortunately the target did not arrive, and a thick fog developed that would have frustrated any action. Calvão returned to operations on the Cacheu River, when new information indicated that the target had been delayed and would now arrive on 7 March. Calvão had to move quickly to re-establish the operation as 'Nebulosa 2'. He met a handpicked and specially-briefed team of fuzileiros at the Bigene airfield on the 5th at 1500, and within four hours all had returned to Bissau, were on board the LFG *Lira* (P 361) and under way. *Lira* arrived at its station on the 6th in the early hours of the morning. Two rubber boats were put into the water, and eight fuzileiros embarked and departed *Lira* at 0300 for the mouth of the Inxanche. They were guided by its radar until contact was lost at a range of about 3,500 meters. After that, they followed the same route as in 'Nebulosa 1' and proceeded slowly with the motors muffled to avoid detection. Guided only by compass and helped by a flood tide, the force found Calebe once more and backed the boats into the mangrove opening that had been made in August and that had remained undetected by the enemy. Indeed, there remained two sacks

of combat rations from the earlier operation.

By 0800 the sea began to ebb, and within two hours the tide had receded to the point that the two boats were grounded and immobilized. By 1600, the tide began to flood and by 1730, the boats were completely afloat. Towards 1800, as twilight came, the boats eased to the opening to be ready for action. After an hour, voices and the splash of paddles guiding a canoe were heard nearby. Minutes later at 1910, engine noise was heard coming from an upstream bearing of 070 degrees magnetic and increasing in intensity. Within 20 minutes, the unmistakable silhouette of the motor launch *Bandim* emerged from the dusk with only a dim, shielded wheelhouse light readily visible. Calvão ordered the motors started and the boats readied to spring the ambush. When they rushed from their hiding place, the first boat took station astern of the target, and the second, a position on its starboard amidships. The first boat immediately fired a bazooka at about 150 meters' range, but it hit short of the target in the anxiety of the moment.[91] Meanwhile, the fuzileiros opened fire with their MG-42 machine gun. The *Bandim* responded with light automatic weapons fire and turned sharply for the sanctuary on the left bank of the river. The boats maneuvered rapidly to maintain their attack positions, and on the third try the bazooka rocket made solid contact with the *Bandim*.[92] The vicious running firefight with the *Bandim* continued with another bazooka hit that disabled its steering and reduced it to circling. It ultimately entered a narrow estuary opposite Calebe, disappeared from view and ran hard aground. The fuzileiros pursued the *Bandim* into the firth, delivered another bazooka hit and when within 10 meters, unloosed a barrage of hand grenades. Enemy automatic weapons fire erupted from the mangroves and was returned with a blast of MG-42 fire by the fuzileiros who were approaching the target.[93]

On boarding the *Bandim*, the fuzileiros discovered six enemy dead. Of these, one was at the entrance to the engine room and another in the pilot house amid the destroyed engine telegraph. The fuzileiros attempted to refloat the vessel, but the engine could not be reversed. The gear lever was blocked with debris from the damage, and a broken fuel line gushed gasoline everywhere. The engine was then stopped, and the fuzileiros considered the idea of towing the prize back to the *Lira*. Theoretically, a line could be attached to the *Bandim* with the two rubber boats acting as tugs. Unfortunately, events conspired against such a plan, as the tide would turn shortly at 2030 and leave the vessel hard aground before the fuzileiros could act. Facing mounting obstacles to the preservation option, Calvão decided to destroy the *Bandim*. Accordingly, gasoline was liberally spread throughout the vessel and lit as the fuzileiros departed. It began burningly slowly, and it was only when the fuzileiros had reached the center of the river that a muffled explosion was heard and flames began to reach high into the night. When the fuzileiros reached the appointed rendezvous point for *Lira* at 2200, the burning *Bandim* remained clearly visible.[94] The destruction of the *Bandim* and the death of its six crewmen threw the enemy into confusion, as judged by its intercepted and deciphered radio traffic.

In the space of six months, two key PAIGC motor vessels had been destroyed and its logistical capability on the frontier dealt a substantial blow. The reduced PAIGC ability to supply its operations in Guiné would perforce reduce its military activity. These missions had exposed

Comandante Alpoim Calvão being awarded the Order of the Tower and Sword by the President of the Republic – Admiral Américo Tomás – in the Terreiro do Paço, Lisbon on 10 June 1971 for his actions in '*Mar Verde*'. (Source: Central Archive of the Navy)

Table 5

'*Mar Verde*' Team Objectives

Ship	Team	Objective	Team Composition
Bombarda	Alfa	Presidential Palace Sékou Touré	FLING
Bombarda	Bravo	Ministry of Interior	FLING
Bombarda	Charlie	Police directorate	FLING
Bombarda	Delta	Executive residences	FLING
Bombarda	Echo	Police barracks	FLING
Bombarda	Foxtrot	*La Paternelle* (Cuban contingent)	FLING
Bombarda	Golf	Post Office Telephone Exchange	FLING
Bombarda	Hotel	National radio station	FLING
Montante	India	Electric grid	FLING & African Commandos (10 men)
Montante	Mike	Camp Samory Chief of Staff Defense	FLING & African Commandos (50 men)
Montante	Oscar	Republican Guard	FLING & African Commandos (40 men)
Bombarda	Papa	Isthmus between Conakry and airport	African Commandos
Hydra	Sierra	Airport	African Commandos (44 men)
Orion	Victor	Fast patrol boats	Fuzileiros (14 men + guide)
Cassiopeia & Dragão	Zulu	Villa Silly de S. Tomé S. Touré residence	DFE 21 (22 men)
Cassiopeia & Dragão	Zulu	PAIGC Headquarters	DFE 21 (22 men)
Cassiopeia & Dragão	Zulu	*La Montaigne* Prison	DFE 21

Sources: Alpoim Calvão, *De Conakry ao M.D.L.P.* [From Conakry to the M.D.L.P.] (Lisbon: Editorial Intervenção, 1976) and António Luís Marinho, *Operação Mar Verde* [Operation Green Sea] (Lisbon: Temas e Debates, 2006).

a glaring PAIGC vulnerability. Its logistical sea lines of communication from Conakry to the frontier were open to aggressive interdiction, as traffic was not protected en route by either armed escort or air cover, and simply relied on international law and crewmen with small arms to defend it.

Following '*Nebulosa*', Calvão had conceived the idea of neutralizing the PAIGC sea operations by sinking its key vessels in Conakry Harbor with limpet mines. In principle, Spínola approved the bold proposal, although it remained largely in the conceptual stage, as the details had yet to be resolved. The concept of the mission, which came to be codenamed '*Mar Verde*' ('Green Sea'), was to send a raiding party from Guiné by sea to Conakry under cover of darkness and to undertake such operations there that would shatter both the ability of the PAIGC to continue its assault on Guiné and the support of Conakry for the PAIGC. The primary mission objectives were to free 26 prisoners, destroy the fast patrol boats of the PAIGC and Republic of Guiné in the port, and disable the six to eight Guinean MIG-15 and MIG-17 jet fighter aircraft at the airport. Secondary objectives would be addressed as opportunity allowed. Destruction of the fast patrol boats and the aircraft was necessary primarily as a defensive measure, because the Portuguese task force would be vulnerable returning to Guiné in daylight on the open ocean. The Portuguese vessels were considerably slower than the enemy boats, were more lightly armed

and lacked effective anti-air defenses. Portuguese air cover from its primary base of Bissau in Guiné did not extend to Conakry, and thus the returning vessels could not be protected during their exposed daylight leg. Consequently, to pre-empt enemy pursuit and a sure disaster, its offensive capability must be neutralized in the port and at the airfield of Conakry. The entire operation relied on the shock of complete initial surprise to enable the relatively small and unprotected Portuguese force to gain the immediate initiative and realize these three vital objectives.

The weekend of 22 November proved ideal for '*Mar Verde*', given the moon phase, predicted tide height, anticipated seasonal winds and other local conditions. These circumstances would not again be propitious for some months. The raiding force was composed of approximately 400 men that included DFE 21 and various personnel from fuzileiro units specifically chosen for this operation. The task force of assault ships reached Conakry in the early hours of the morning and launched the operation. During these early hours, the prisoners were freed and control of the sea and air established. Having then achieved his primary objectives, Calvão decided to terminate the operation and recovered his forces on board the vessels by 0900. His losses were three dead and nine wounded. Conversely, Sékou Touré had lost over 500 troops and many civilians, and presided over a partially destroyed and disorganized city.[95] By 1030, Calvão's task force had stood out of Conakry and made its turn north.

From the strictly military point of view, 'Mar Verde' was a success. It was the first of its kind ever undertaken by Portugal, and it proved once again the capabilities and effectiveness of the sailor-fuzileiro team. They had stormed a bastion in a city relatively far from their base of operations and relied on surprise to achieve the success necessary for a safe withdrawal. It had been an ingenious plan that ably addressed the limited resources, the unique operational security requirements and an incomplete intelligence picture.

Subsequently, Portugal became a controversial member of NATO, but the real difficulty came at the international level – and in going to Conakry, Lisbon had tended to forget the broader picture.[96] Spínola did not agree, and many years later he confirmed that in his opinion, it was mostly overblown.[97]

The Final Years

'Mar Verde' did not end the war, nor did it lessen its intensity for the fuzileiros. In the north, Spínola continued with his counter-penetration strategy – and in the words of one fuzileiro, Sambuiá became the 'graveyard of fuzileiros'. As Talhadas describes it, month after month from mid-1970, there was an increase in enemy activity, and his unit – DFE 12 – entered a period of frenetic operational intensity.[98] During this period, DFE 12 assaulted enemy encampments in the interior of the territory and conducted armed actions against villages where enemy groups were bivouacking overnight. Primarily, however, DFE 12 operated along the Cacheu. Its actions jumped from one bank to the other and encompassed an extensive area, the southern part of which had become depopulated during the war. For the fuzileiro, the operational panorama expanded enormously from what it had been in the 1960s. Within the COP 3 area of responsibility, the only intervention forces were the 'fuzos', so now they were responsible for the entire length of the Cacheu within the COP 3 zone. The north had become the land of war, and the fuzileiros on all operations now avoided any road or track, as it would inevitably hold the potential for an ambush or booby-trap. Instead they traveled in the forest or through low grassy areas – a procedure that took more time, but was infinitely more secure.[99] This practice inevitably caused them to advance slowly and cautiously and resulted in a pace of about one kilometer an hour. Only in extreme cases did they call for air support, as an aircraft buzzing around would alert the enemy to the fuzileiro presence and inevitably compromise the desired surprise.[100]

DFE 12 conducted strikes at will in areas next to the border or even across the border into Senegal, the most spectacular of which was breaching the PAIGC base of Sanou (Sano in Portuguese) some two kilometers into Casamance. Sanou was a PAIGC rearguard and logistics base situated about halfway between Cossé and Tubacuta (approximately two kilometers into Senegal), and somewhere between frontier markers 131 and 132. It was from here that the

PAIGC organized thrusts into Guiné and many times attacked the village of Barro.[101] In this strike, the detachment crossed the border at Bucaur towards Sanou after transiting an area of lush grass and a swampy bolanha. Dawn brought a half-light, and in it the section leader next to Talhadas bumped into a sleeping enemy sentinel, who in the shock of being suddenly awoken – and seeing a bearded fuzileiro in front of him – was 'frightened out of his wits'. He leaped up and ran madly away in a panic. This obligated the lead men in the section to pursue the sentinel, as he would potentially arouse the sleeping enemy. Suddenly in this confusion, the detachment became fragmented. The first section abruptly entered the base where the PAIGC troops and the population slept and were taken under fire at the same instant. Suddenly, it was practically man-to-man combat.[102]

Perhaps the most astonishing event occurred in the middle of the fight, when the guide Bacar Camará recognized some of the people as members of his family or clan who were refugees in Senegal. Bacar was the headman in the village of Bigene and had seen many of his extended family cross into Senegal to escape the fighting. Bacar began to run toward them – hailing them and calling them by name. This event caused some confusion, and a number of the fuzileiros fired in their direction believing that Bacar's kin were the enemy.[103] The PAIGC troops returned a withering and continuous fire with small arms and bazookas. Clearly they were protecting something or somebody important and attempting to withdraw with it, perhaps their leaders. After about an hour of shooting, it became eerily quiet. The fuzileiros searched for the enemy and found three dead uniformed insurgents. There was a great deal of blood on the ground, presumably from the wounded who had been carried away in the withdrawal. What was notable about this action was the enemy retreat with its important weapons. The fuzileiros were unable to capture the recoilless rifles, for instance, that were so important to the enemy. In the end, there were only the same old wheeled heavy machine guns remaining. In searching, the fuzileiros found great quantities of grenades, munitions and enough uniforms to outfit a company of the enemy. Important to intelligence were the many documents discovered. Finally on departing, the fuzileiros burned the enemy huts and matériel that they were unable to carry and headed for Ganturé by way of Bigene.[104] As there was no air support, the fuzileiros were unable to conduct a rapid pursuit, for they would be blind and subject to counterattack with mortars and recoilless rifles.

From 1970 onward, Spínola had attempted to reduce the military capacity of the PAIGC, tilting the balance in Portuguese favor. By 1972, conditions were ripe for negotiations, and at the end of April he had his initial conversations with a Senegalese minister to explain his concept of Guinean independence. Contact was initiated with Cabral; however, with his assassination in January 1973, the war in Guiné entered a waiting period – during which there seemed to be a general expectation that some event would end the conflict. The war labored on until 25 April 1974, when middle-ranking Portuguese officers effected a coup and toppled the government in Lisbon. Guiné received its independence the following year.

(Endnotes)

1. António José Telo, *História da Marinha Portuguesa: Homens, Doutrinas e Organização, 1824–1974* (Tomo I) [History of the Portuguese Navy: Men, Doctrine and Organization, 1824–1974 (Volume I)] (Lisbon: Academia de Marinha, 1999), p.575.
2. Ibid.
3. José Alberto Lopes Carvalheira, "Guiné: Esquadrilha de Lanchas e Outros Navios" [Guiné: Squadron of Patrol Boats and Other Ships], in the unpublished collection *Participação da Armada na Defesa das Províncias Ultramarinas* [Participation of the Navy in the Defense of the Overseas Provinces], TMs [photocopy] (Lisbon: Ministério de Marinha, 1972), p.5.
4. Al J. Venter, *Portugal's Insurgent War, The Campaign for Africa* (Cape Town: John Malherbe, 1973), p.13.
5. José Talhadas, *Memórias de um guerriro colonial* [Memories of a colonial warrior] (Lisbon: Âncora Editora, 2009), p.71.
6. Estado-Maior do Exército, *Resenha Histórico-Militar das Campanhas de África, Vol. III, Dispositivo das Nossas Forças Guiné* [Historical Military Report of the African Campaigns, Vol. III, Disposition of Our Forces in Guiné] (Lisbon: Estado-Maior do Exército, 1989), pp.20–21.
7. Talhadas, *Memórias*, p.71.
8. Ibid., p.72.
9. John P. Cann, *Contra-Subversão em África: Como os Portugueses Fizeram a Guerra, 1961–1974* [Counter-Subversion in Africa: The Portuguese Way of War, 1961–1974] (Lisbon: Prefácio, 2005), p.25.
10. Telo, *História da Marinha Portuguesa*, p.576.
11. Cann, *Contra-Subversão*, p.25.
12. René Pélissier, *Le Naufrage des Caravelles, Etudes sur la Fin de l'Empire Portugais (1961–1975)* (Orgeval: Editions Pélissier, 1979), p.18.
13. Estado-Maior do Exército, Vol. III, p.17.
14. Ibid., p.27.
15. Pélissier, *Le Naufrage des Caravelles*, p.208.
16. Thomas H. Hendriksen, "Portugal in Africa: Comparative Notes on Counterinsurgency," *Orbis* (Summer 1977), p.404.
17. Estado-Maior do Exército, *Resenha Histórico-Militar das Campanhas de África, Vol. I, Enquadramento Geral* [Historical Military Report of the African Campaigns, Vol. I, General Framework] (Lisbon: Estado-Maior do Exército, 1988), pp.331–334.
18. Talhadas, *Memórias*, p.73.
19. Ibid.
20. Ibid., p.74.
21. Ibid., p.79.
22. José Alberto Lopes Carvalheira, "Acção da Marinha em Águas Interiores, 1961–1971" [Naval Operations in Inland Waters], in the unpublished collection *Participação da Armada na Defesa das Províncias Ultramarinas* [Participation of the Navy in the Defense of the Overseas Provinces], TMs [photocopy] (Lisbon: Ministério de Marinha, 1972), pp.1–2.
23. Hortelão, Baêna and Sousa, *Alpoim Calvão*, p.61.
24. Lopes Carvalheira, "Guiné: Esquadrilha de Lanchas e Outros Navios," p.4.
25. Eurico Nelson de Campos Marques Pinto, *capitão de mar e guerra*, interview by the author, 6 February 2003, Lisbon.
26. Carlos Encaração Gomes, *capitão de frigate (fuzileiro)*, interview by the author, 5 February 2003, Lisbon.
27. Ibid.
28. Ibid.
29. Ibid.
30. Telo, *História da Marinha Portuguesa*, p.580.
31. Hortelão, Baêna and Sousa, *Alpoim Calvão*, p.67.
32. Ibid.
33. Ibid.
34. Luís Sanches de Baêna, *Fuzileiros: Factos e Feitos na Guerra de África, 1961/1974* [Marines: Deeds and Feats in the African War, 1961/1974], vol. 3, *Crónica dos Feitos da Guiné* [Chronicle of the Feats of Guiné] (Lisbon: Comissão Cultural da Marinha–INAPA, 2006), p.23.
35. Guilherme Almor de Alpoim Calvão, *De Conakry ao M.D.L.P.* [From Conakry to the M.D.L.P.] (Lisbon: Editorial Intervenção, 1976), p.52
36. Guilherme Almor de Alpoim Calvão, correspondence with the author, 9 May 2005, Cascais.
37. Baêna, *Fuzileiros*, vol. 3, p.21.
38. Hortelão, Baêna and Sousa, *Alpoim Calvão*, p.69.
39. Ibid., p.62.
40. Aniceto Afonso and Carlos de Matos Gomes, *Guerra Colonial* [Colonial War] (Lisbon: Notícias, 2000), p.79.
41. Hortelão, Baêna and Sousa, *Alpoim Calvão*, p.71.
42. Ibid., p.72.
43. Ibid., p.73. This is an expression linked to the Spanish-American War, when President William McKinley decided to establish contact with the Cuban rebel leader General Calixto García, whom he thought would be a valuable ally in case of war with Spain. Captain Andrew Rowan, an expert on the island, was selected in early 1898 to travel to Cuba with a message from McKinley and seek out García, who was hiding in the Oriente Mountains. According to Rowan, it was the most perilous journey he had ever undertaken; a journey fraught with danger at every turn, particularly the danger of death at the hands of a Spanish firing squad. After many adventures, Rowan eventually found his way and was able to meet with García in his hideout. He established a rapport with García and discovered that he was eager to cooperate with Americans in fighting the Spanish. Rowan's return to Washington was less arduous, and in 1899 Elbert Hubbard wrote and published a passage entitled *A Message to Garcia* that described the search for García, extolled the virtues of Rowan and lauded his reliability and competence under the most trying circumstances. For industrial and military leaders, the message had enormous appeal, and they ordered millions of copies of the text to distribute to their workers and soldiers. This catapulted the book to best-seller status and led to its translation into a number of languages and distribution abroad – thus to 'deliver a message to García' became the definition of a nearly impossible task being completed successfully under the most trying of circumstances, and was a popular and well-understood expression with the Portuguese military during its campaigns in the *ultramar*.
44. Ibid., p.77.
45. Ibid., p.79.

46. Ibid., p.82.
47. Ibid., p.83.
48. Afonso and Matos Gomes, *Guerra Colonial*, p.81.
49. João Bernardo "Nino" Vieira, correspondence with Rui Demba Djassi and Domingos Ramos, 3 March 1964, undisclosed PAIGC base in Southern Guiné, typewritten transcript furnished by Guilherme Almor de Alpoim Calvão in correspondence with the author, 9 May 2005, Cascais.
50. Afonso and Matos Gomes, *Guerra Colonial*, p.81.
51. Guilherme Almor de Alpoim Calvão, correspondence with the author, 9 May 2005, Cascais.
52. Afonso and Matos Gomes, *Guerra Colonial*, p.81.
53. Hortelão, Baêna and Sousa, *Alpoim Calvão*, p.95.
54. Mongua is a place name and the site of an action between indigenous troops and invading Germans in World War One in the Baixo-Cunene region of Angola.
55. Hortelão, Baêna and Sousa, *Alpoim Calvão*, pp.106–107.
56. Baêna, *Fuzileiros*, vol. 3, p.53.
57. Ibid., p.109.
58. Ibid., p.54.
59. Ibid., p.62.
60. Hortelão, Baêna and Sousa, *Alpoim Calvão*, p.110.
61. Baêna, *Fuzileiros*, vol. 3, p.53.
62. Ibid., p.64.
63. Ibid., p.65.
64. Ibid., p.66.
65. John P. Cann, "Low-Intensity Conflict, Insurgency, Terrorism and Revolutionary War," in *Palgrave Advances in Modern Military History*, ed. Matthew Hughes and William J. Philpott (New York: Palgrave Macmillan, 2006), pp.114–116.
66. Baêna, *Fuzileiros*, vol. 3, p.76.
67. Talhadas, *Memórias*, p.77.
68. Telo, *História da Marinha Portuguesa*, p.587.
69. Baêna, *Fuzileiros*, vol. 3, p.107.
70. Talhadas, *Memórias*, pp.84.
71. Ibid.
72. Ibid.
73. Ibid., pp.85–86.
74. Ibid., p.86.
75. Baêna, *Fuzileiros*, vol. 3, pp.103–111.
76. Admiral Nuno Vieira Matias, deposition from Oral History Project, July 1999, as quoted in Baêna, *Fuzileiros*, vol. 3, pp.114–115.
77. Ibid.
78. Ibid.
79. Ibid.
80. Baêna, *Fuzileiros*, vol. 3, p.144.
81. Ibid.
82. Guilherme Almor de Alpoim Calvão, *De Conakry ao M.D.L.P.* [From Conakry to the M.D.L.P.] (Lisbon: Editorial Intervenção, 1976), p.13.
83. Ibid., p.57.
84. Ibid., pp.57–58.
85. LFG *Sagitário* (P 1131) was one of the final two vessels of the *Argos* class launches and was completed in September 1965 at the Arsenal do Alfeite, Lisbon. The other was LFG *Centauro* (P 1130).
86. Calvão, *De Conakry ao M.D.L.P.*, p.59.
87. José Freire Antunes, *A Guerra de África 1961–1974* [The African War 1961–1974] (Lisbon: Temas e Debates, 1996), p.513.
88. Calvão, *De Conakry ao M.D.L.P.*, p.59.
89. Ibid.
90. Abou Camaná, an ex-PAIGC sailor, was enlisted in the fuzileiros as part of the Portuguese policy of rehabilitating former insurgents. He was later assigned to DFE 21, a *Destacamento de Fuzileiros Especiais Africanos* (Detachment of African Special Fuzileiros), which was established in February 1970. He was to participate in 'Mar Verde' and be awarded the Cruz de Guerra for his heroism.
91. Calvão, *De Conakry ao M.D.L.P.*, p.60.
92. The M20 bazooka is a World War Two-vintage 88.9 mm rocket-propelled grenade launcher with a maximum range of 800 meters and a recommended moving target acquisition range of 185 meters.
93. Calvão, *De Conakry ao M.D.L.P.*, p.62.
94. Calvão, *De Conakry ao M.D.L.P.*, p.63.
95. Ibid., p.64.
96. José Manuel Saraiva, "Asslto a Conakry" [Assault on Conakry], *Revista do Expresso* (23 November 1996), p.104.
97. Antunes, "Calvão evoca Conakry," p.104.
98. José Pedro Castanheira, "Ao Serviço de Spínola e Marcelo" [In the Service of Spínola and Marcelo], *Expresso* (20 September 1997), pp.28–30.
99. Talhadas, *Memórias*, p.187.
100. Ibid., p.199.
101. Ibid.
102. Ibid., p.200.
103. Ibid., p.201.
104. Ibid.
105. Ibid., p.202.

CHAPTER 4
NIASSA AND THE INDIAN OCEAN

The Northern Mozambican border with Tanzania runs the length of the Rovuma River – some 708 kilometers from its mouth on the Indian Ocean to its confluence with the Messinge River – and then along a parallel of latitude an additional 48 kilometers west to the shore of Lake Niassa, a total of 756 kilometers. The entire riverine frontier runs through some of the most inaccessible, remote and rugged tropical bush country in Africa, and represented a porous border and easy opportunity for insurgent infiltration. In a classic interior line defense, the army was given responsibility for the security of this river border and addressed the problem by establishing a series of fixed posts at intervals along the river, and conducted land patrols from these posts to police the frontier. The line was anchored on each end by water. On the eastern end, the navy was assigned coastal patrol responsibility in the Indian Ocean over an area that extended from the mouth of the Rovuma southward, across the Bay of Tungue and as far as Ibo Island, a distance of approximately 120 miles. From 1966 onward, the navy likewise anchored the western flank and initiated its policing of Lake Niassa.[1] The naval strategy in pursuing this two-fold 'bookend' plan was to prevent the insurgents from outflanking the army and extending the conflict beyond the two northern frontier districts of Niassa and Cabo Delgado and into Téte and Zambézia. In Niassa, the navy bent to this task with a will using the potent and tested combination of launches and fuzileiros. In the Indian Ocean, there was a more varied array of vessels in the frigates, corvettes, launches and fuzileiros to secure the eastern flank. Both were remarkably successful, despite the limited resources.

The Insurgent Problem

Of the three theaters of operations, Mozambique was the final one – and probably would not have developed as such but for the granting of independence to Tanzania in 1961. It was the emergence of Julius Nyerere, first as its Premier and later in 1962 as its President, that was the most telling development, as he was an ardent nationalist who was passionately committed to supporting and providing a home for African liberation movements. These included the African National Congress (ANC) and the Pan African Congress (PAC) of South Africa, the Zimbabwe African National Union (ZANU) and Robert Mugabe in their struggle to unseat the white regime in Southern Rhodesia (now Zimbabwe), and most importantly to our story, FRELIMO. FRELIMO began with a disorganized force of uncertain strength and by the early 1970s, had an active force of about 7,200 regulars and 2,400 popular militia, and these operated from a network of bases on the Tanzanian side of the border.[2] The primary one was Nachinghea, and depots were built at Songea, Tunduru and Lindi. There were also five bases next to the border for staging incursions: Mbamba Bay, Chamba, Lukwila, Newala and Mtwara.[3]

FRELIMO initiated hostilities on the evening of 24 September 1964 with an assault on the residence and secretariat of the small administrative post (or *posto*) of Cobué in the Niassa district. The following day, the LFP *Castor* (P 580) was fired upon while on patrol in Lake Niassa, and the *posto* in Chai, on the southern edge of the Makonde plateau in the Cabo Delgado district, was assaulted. Later in December, the *posto* in Olivença, just north and east of Cobué, was attacked. A FRELIMO prisoner taken there revealed that FRELIMO was using N'Gombe, a remote settlement in North-Western Niassa, as a base. Accordingly, the navy sent *Castor* and a section of fuzileiros from CF 2 to conduct an amphibious operation against it on 5 January, and the operation managed to consume three days, as the insurgents fought to prevent the small security force from landing.[4] The fuzileiros were able to come ashore only four at a time in a small aluminum boat, and thus the ability to concentrate force and maneuver against the enemy was limited. *Castor* had to return to Metangula for reinforcements in the midst of the operation and lacked either an Oerlikon or a Dreyse automatic deck-mounted weapon to support the force ashore. The available airpower, a Lockheed PV-2 Harpoon and two North American T-6 Harvards at Vila Cabral, remained grounded and unable to help because of the weather, as it was the rainy season. Eventually the Portuguese prevailed, and Radio Tanzania at Dar-es-Salaam confirmed two days after the operation that FRELIMO had suffered eight killed and many gravely wounded. Clearly the Portuguese needed a more substantial, skilled and coordinated force to address the threat on Lake Niassa.

Naval Commitment

The Naval Command Mozambique (*Comando Naval de Moçambique*, or CNM) was created in 1957 at the same time as the one in Angola and was initially preoccupied with the construction of basic naval infrastructure. Early on it built the headquarters in Lourenço Marques, radio stations at Machava (Lourenço Marques) and later (between 1964 and 1965) in Beira, Nacala, Metangula on Lake Niassa and Porto Amélia on the Indian Ocean, as well as offices in Lourenço Marques and Beira, and port installations in Metangula and Porto Amélia.[5] From October 1962, CF 2 was deployed to Lourenço Marques to guard naval facilities, and because of a lack of DFEs, initiated its own training for counterinsurgency operations. Personnel so trained were formed into two platoons: one deployed to Cobué and the other to Metangula, both on Lake Niassa. In the spring of 1964, *Castor* arrived at the Indian Ocean port of Nacala and was transferred to Lake Niassa in the fall of that year. The next year, significant forces began to arrive and be deployed, as FRELIMO activity began to intensify in the north. Naval forces sought to intercept infiltrators while they were still at sea or on the lake and vulnerable, for once ashore, they easily melted into an intimidated population, or sought refuge in the difficult terrain and tended to become 'invisible'. Developing an interdiction

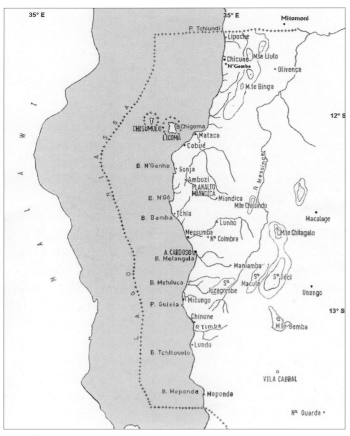

Lake Niassa.
(Source: Modified by the author from a Portuguese briefing map)

capability required the establishment of a significant naval presence first on Lake Niassa and later on, the Indian Ocean. The value of such forces cannot be understated in frustrating an enemy.

Niassa Operations

Lake Niassa is an inland sea. Its water is quite pure, and it has no tides. It does have about a five-meter seasonal change in level from its May-high to its December-low because of its various underground rivers and seasonal rainfall. Conditions are similar to those in the ocean in that they can easily become untenable for small craft with high winds from the north, consequent heavy seas, and waves reaching three meters in height. Such conditions, of course, affected the enemy too. The FRELIMO insurgents in their canoes or Tanzanian vessels hoped to avoid naval contact altogether in their transit to remote areas of infiltration. Here again, the potent and effective combination of launches and fuzileiros would have to dominate the littorals to stem this infiltration and disrupt insurgent use of the lake. This disruption would force the insurgents to go by land across difficult, daunting and mountainous terrain and not by the easier water route – thus FRELIMO would lose the logistical battle in supplying its forces in Mozambique, and its strategic reach would be substantially limited.

Security operations on the lake centered on the primary naval base of Metangula and its satellite Cobué to the north. The installation at Metangula was alternatively called 'Vila Augusto Cardoso' during Portuguese ownership and was named after the first naval commander to explore Mozambique. It was a well-ordered and immaculate facility

A patrol launch on Lake Niassa showing the weather conditions that could arise with its high winds and consequent rough seas.
(Source: Personal archive of Kaúlza de Arriaga)

A rubber boat with its fuzileiro complement making its way towards the shore of Lake Niassa. (Source: Escola de Fuzileiros)

A rubber boat with a fuzileiro element preparing for a landing; note the squad leader examining his map in preparation for landing. (Source: Escola de Fuzileiros)

sited on a secure peninsula, together with a lighthouse and an airstrip. From August 1967, it supported four *Júpiter* class launches, four medium landing craft, three small landing craft, one company of naval fuzileiros and two detachments of special fuzileiros: one in Cobué and the other at Metangula. There was likewise a radio station that served as a vital part of the worldwide naval communications system, and an army infantry company encamped nearby in more reduced circumstances.

Metangula was considerably isolated by its vulnerable road link that resulted in a slow and unresponsive logistics system based on supplying the base by truck. There was consequently an annoying shortage of almost everything. The food was particularly terrible, and there was no significant native game to augment the rations. Fishing proved a disappointment as well. As time went on, the lack of variation in the meals wore on the men. Rarely was there a supply of fresh produce. Bacalhau, tuna, mackerel and more types of canned meat formed the basis of the available supplies. As fuzileiro Lieutenant Raúl Patrício Leitão noted: 'What could be more important to us than the substantial improvement of our menus? Fresh vegetables! Eggs from perhaps a dozen chickens wandering the yard!'[6] On top of the inconvenience of monotonous food, insects abounded in the hot, tropical climate, descending in swarms on the fuzileiros.

Cobué, located some 50 miles to the north of Metangula and opposite the Malawian islands of

Licoma and Chisumulo, was the site of an old mission with its imposing but rather plain church. It had been founded and was still run by Italian priests, although the conflict severely reduced its operation. The village itself was a planned development associated with the mission, but its population had abandoned it almost totally with the advent of war. The vacant buildings accordingly were converted to accommodate a DFE, a CF platoon and a forward naval command post.[7] Like Metangula, it was relatively spartan. In contrast, however, it was near the Tanzanian border and consequently in the midst of insurgent activity.

Patrols were conducted along the entire 115-mile coastline, which was based first on the need to demonstrate a presence, and second, on intelligence ranging from the specific to the very general. Intelligence was gained from three sources: prisoner interrogation, reconnaissance flights and routine operations.[8] The normal patrol profile would entail the sortie of a launch from either Metangula or Cobué with a platoon of fuzileiros embarked, which would remain at sea for five days. During this period, the fuzileiros would be landed from time to time to conduct foot patrols, ambushes and cordon and search operations, and to gather intelligence from the population. At the beginning of a patrol, the LF would assume station about 1,000 meters from shore with its radar operating for navigation and identification of local water traffic. If a suspicious contact were identified either through radar or by lookouts, it was investigated. The patrol would continue to an opportune landing site to disembark the fuzileiros for their foot patrol. Once the site was identified – and this might be done based on intelligence, experience or simply a suspicion of enemy activity – the fuzileiros would be put ashore in their rubber boats or from a landing craft. When they were ashore, the launch would stand ready to support and assist. The patrol would adjust its tactics to be covert or overt, depending on whether or not it was thought the landing had been observed and was known to the population. The launches were noisy, so it was generally assumed that FRELIMO knew when operations were afoot, but there were also deception techniques similar to those on the Zaire to help conceal the exact nature of naval activity. At the conclusion of the five-day cruise, the launch crew would recover its fuzileiro contingent, and all would return to base for a three-day rest.

At times, these missions suffered from rushed (and thus incomplete) planning. This resulted oftentimes in having the fuzileiros walk great distances and only occasionally surprising FRELIMO. FRELIMO bases were a distance from the lakeside and on high ground in the mountains to the east. This meant that unless the enemy ventured from his retreat, the fuzileiros had to seek him out. If he were found and engaged, then subsequent missions would seek to exploit this experience. If prisoners were taken, then their interrogation would shape future mission planning and execution. Indeed, the interrogation of prisoners proved a valuable source of intelligence not only for the precise location of enemy bases and his intentions, but his morale and tactical thinking as well. Reconnaissance flights would be used to confirm and revise the intelligence picture.[9]

The enemy covered the coast well with sentinels and was generally able to detect a landing and avoid being surprised. These sentinels also tracked the progress of the fuzileiros once a landing had been detected. This was not, however, always the case. The fuzileiros' most difficult threat in Niassa was the presence of mines. Whenever the fuzileiros were landing or embarking, they would carefully probe the beach and establish a clear trail across the sand to the bush. They would use only this sanitized pathway coming and going. In the bush they always avoided trails, as these too were inevitably mined.[10]

As the security situation deteriorated, DFE 1 was deployed to the territory in November 1965 and installed at Porto Amélia, where it conducted operations in Cabo Delgado. In January 1966, the DFE was relocated to Lake Niassa, where it experienced enemy resistance in its probes, but it was an enemy who fled on contact with the fuzileiros. On 13 January in Operation 'Teimosia' ('Persistence'), DFE 12 – reinforced with a section of CF 6 – for the first time used a war dog on patrol. As the fuzileiros progressed along a trail, they encountered seven of the enemy who opened fire immediately, but quickly fled with the onrush of the attacking dog. The dog's comportment on patrol was impeccable.[11]

In March, the fuzileiros rotated assignments: DFE 5 moved to Cobué, DFE 12 to Porto Amélia and DFE 1 to Metangula. DFE 5 established a temporary base at Lipoche near the Tanzanian border and patrolled the area to disrupt FRELIMO traffic attempting to cross the lake. Operations from Cobué were initially difficult in that the care of the wounded was primitive. The rations were thin and tasteless, as resupplying Cobué in its remoteness was haphazard. Electricity was non-existent, which meant that food and medicine could not be preserved. There was no doctor.[12] Further, the combat ration given to each fuzileiro was an unpalatable combination of cans of sardines, pieces of crisp-roasted pork fat and chocolate milk, which when combined with an unappetizing fruit bar, generally caused such a thirst that the best option was often to go on patrol with an empty pack in the hope of finding one of the frequent fields of cassava or corn and then gnawing the grains from the cob to cheat hunger for a bit. The most important thing for each operation was to have two or three canteens filled with water in the event that it did not rain.[13]

By the end of 1966, DFE 5 was installed at Porto Amélia, DFE 8 in Metangula and DFE 12 in Cobué. The New Year opened auspiciously when a native Mozambican fled from his life in the bush and presented himself to the authorities. He was more than willing to act as a guide and to lead the fuzileiros to his former FRELIMO base. Accordingly, DFE 12 departed Cobué in the landing craft and, after being put ashore in the targeted area, was immediately taken under fire from a distance with the clear enemy intent of frustrating progress to its objective. At a point about 200 meters from the enemy encampment, the DFE was ambushed by an entrenched and heavily-armed enemy who delivered machine gun fire at a consistently high rate. Recovering, the DFE put the enemy to flight and found itself opposite a typical military encampment: 12 huts around a square or parade, and five others about a hundred meters distant. This was the enemy base of Tchia. The fuzileiros found evidence of meals being prepared and sums of money. The defense of the base included a relatively advanced alarm system with outlying sentinels stationed at a distance to provide adequate warning. There was also a system of tin cans with trip wires to raise the alarm, but this ingenious device proved insufficient to prevent the fuzileiros from destroying the base. Leitão describes the early experiences of DFE 8 deployed to Metangula in late December 1966: the DFE was divided into three platoons, or combat groups, of about 25 men each, and each began its acclimation with 'learning' operations in January. Leitão commanded the third of the three groups, and as his section patrolled in the field, his fuzileiros seemed to be regularly but intermittently in contact with FRELIMO elements. The fuzileiros under his command were generally young men of about 18 or 19 years who had joined the navy at 16 and volunteered for this specialty. Indeed, they were an accurate reflection of the *Corpo de Fuzileiros* at large, as it was a young organization with approximately one-third of its members being combat veterans, a potent mix of youth and experience. Leitão's group operated initially in the area of Malawi south of Metangula, but soon he was transferred to Cobué in one of the many personnel rotations designed to provide a change of scenery. It was a time of opportunity, and he was soon face to face with FRELIMO. On 23 March 1967, in one of his initial operations, his combat group was taken by Lieutenant Torres Sobral in a launch to a point a little over 15 miles north of Cobué and put ashore at about 0500 hours just prior to sunrise. There had been no specific indication of enemy activity between Cobué and the Tanzanian border; however, this perception may have been because the FRELIMO elements in the mountains could easily see and hear any approaching Portuguese force and avoid it. The mined roads forced all traffic to move by water, so it was not unusual to see or hear Portuguese launches under way. The Portuguese would take advantage of this activity to make noise or to be silent, depending on the deception scenario. In this case, it was hoped that the noisy launch had not been heard at the early hour and that the enemy remained unaware.

Leitão and his fuzileiros moved over rough ground in the nether light and followed the standard practice of avoiding the tracks and trails, for the insurgents not only mined them, but their shoulders as well. The group walked for an hour and covered about three kilometers over difficult terrain with no particular objective other than simple reconnaissance. As daylight approached, Leitão sought an observation site on the top of a nearby hill. He was enjoying a smoke with his medic, radioman and bodyguard, as the remainder of the group deployed nearby, and in so doing surprised two 12-year-old boys. From their broken Portuguese, Leitão learned that they had left a FRELIMO base without authorization to fish at a nearby lake. According to the youths, the base was about

five miles east of the hill and was divided into two encampments: one containing warriors, and the other, camp followers. There was always a man with a bazooka guarding the base to warn of approaching danger, but then the boys had managed to avoid him in leaving. The boys also described a protective minefield surrounding the base and knew how to negotiate it. Leitão imagined from their description and his knowledge of the area that there might be a dozen or so men in the base and that his fuzileiros could easily handle them. Had he thought that there were more, then he would have called for reinforcements before beginning his march to attack the base.

It took the fuzileiros about two hours to negotiate the irregular terrain and reach the site. The party paused at the top of a hill about 300 meters from the base to take stock and develop a plan of attack. With only 27 men, it would have to be simple. The insurgents were visible through the trees and were unsuspectingly going about their

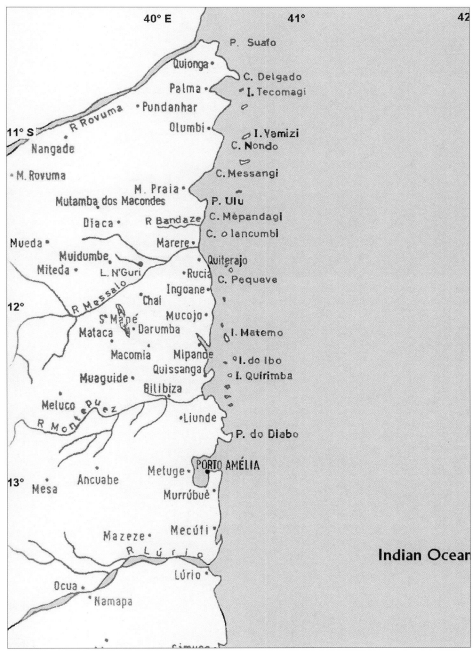

The Indian Ocean and the Quirimbas Archipelago.
(Source: Modified by the author from a Portuguese briefing map)

daily routine in preparation for the noon meal. Leitão planned to leave the two boys, the medic, the radioman, the mortar bearer and a *sepoy* outside the minefield, which the boys had identified, and proceed with the main body in a column through the mines.[14] He would then have his men shift to a line abreast to sweep through the camp, using the perimeter minefield as the anvil in a hammer-and-anvil tactic. Because the terrain and undergrowth limited line-of-sight communication, Leitão briefed his fuzileiros that he would allow five minutes for deployment of the force around the enemy camp. At the end of that time, all would move forward in execution of the attack. No one would fire until he heard Leitão fire.

During the five-minute deployment, Leitão observed that the base was a village surrounded with a series of small fences, and the population appeared relaxed and unsuspecting. He thought this unusual, as he knew that Torres Sobral's launch had been quite noisy in landing his force. Suddenly, about 30 meters from the village, a tree fell unexpectedly. Still no one took notice, as apparently a tree falling in the bush was a routine event. As Leitão began his move forward and neared the village, he realized that his group was hopelessly outnumbered, but it was too late to worry, as the group was committed to attack.

When the assault began, the FRELIMO insurgents were completely surprised and either fled or fell in place during the five-minute fight. In the end, there were about 60 insurgents killed or wounded, and a single fuzileiro wounded. The fuzileiros collected all of the weapons that they could find and lobbed a few mortar rounds into the camp before returning to the lake and the launch. By sunset, the entire party with its captured weapons had returned to Cobué.

There were a number of follow-up raids to the village site in which prisoners were captured and interrogated, and the one nice surprise revealed in the intelligence was that the two boys had not been punished. At Cobué, the prisoners were allowed to build their own village, and it was expanded to 200 people with the subsequent capture of fighters and the relocation of their families. The village became a partial source of local labor and modest crops, and in turn was the recipient of military largess, particularly food and aspirin.

The success of operations was measured by the number of weapons captured rather than insurgents killed or FRELIMO activities disrupted. The aim of this policy was to avoid killing the enemy, who might actually be an unwilling local forced to fight by FRELIMO. Indeed, many Portuguese soldiers were wounded in effecting this policy and trying to maintain good relations with the population. Despite the war, the people trusted the Portuguese and regularly came to their bases to receive medical treatment.

NRP *Cimitarra* (LDG 103) positions itself off the difficult Cabo Delgado Coast with its shoals and reefs to launch a combat group of fuzileiros. (Source: Escola de Fuzileiros)

A combat group of fuzileiros makes its final checks before launching in its rubber boats for the distant Cabo Delgado Coast. Careful preparation is critical, as the clandestine mission will last many days and cannot be supported externally. (Source: Escola de Fuzileiros)

This use of captured weapons as a measure of effectiveness seems to be a strange yardstick in that an almost endless supply was available in Tanzania, and for that matter Guiné, the Congo and Zambia. The lost weapons were easily replaced, but the insurgents themselves required recruitment, training, combat experience and loyalty to be useful. This process of personal development took far longer and was infinitely more complicated than delivering technologically-dated weapons from obsolete and overflowing Communist Bloc stockpiles. Consequently, when surrounded or surprised by Portuguese forces, insurgents would quickly abandon their weapons (with their heavy weight) to increase their mobility in fleeing the fight, and to help in blending with the unarmed population in order to live to fight another day.

Operations continued in this vein and proved extremely effective – so much so that FRELIMO in Niassa found itself stalemated and restricted to an area bounded by Lake Niassa and the Lugenda River in North-West Niassa. The primary difficulty for the fuzileiros became an enemy reduced to a miniscule force – difficult to detect until he suddenly struck. As a result of its failure in Niassa, FRELIMO sought in 1970 to open a Western Front in the district of Tete.[15]

Indian Ocean Operations

In the north-eastern district of Cabo Delgado, the Indian Ocean littoral was characterized by numerous bays and offshore islands that provided excellent entry points for FRELIMO insurgents infiltrating by sea from the north along the coast. The strategy of FRELIMO in this instance was to dominate the littoral of Cabo Delgado and hence control the riverine and littoral populations from whom its fighters hoped to obtain fish and other provisions.[16]

The Portuguese authorities had always maintained a naval presence in the small base at Porto Amélia, where the Maritime Defense Command of Porto Amélia (*Comando da Defesa Marítima de Porto Amélia*, or CDMPA) was headquartered. Its mission was to protect Portuguese sovereign waters and their littorals in its zone, to conduct maritime inspections of transiting craft, to provide civil and military logistical support along the littoral and to participate in joint military operations. Over the years, the CDMPA acquired six permanently-assigned ships with which to execute its responsibilities. One of these spent its time patrolling the Quirimbas Archipelago – a group of offshore islands that stretched between Palma in the north and Porto Amélia in the south – and its primary role was to land fuzileiros in night-time covert operations to disrupt enemy activity. These would be along the coast and generally around the mouth of the Messalo River, which is surrounded by the Quirimbas Islands. These islands were restricted inner waters or narrow seas, and for the frigates or corvettes, navigation through this labyrinthine island chain in darkness presented certain dangers. Charts were inexact, and the currents freakish and unpredictable. The islands were surrounded by coral reefs, and if the ship's radar failed, it was very difficult. Even with perfect radar operation, it was invariably a tense passage for a ship's crew.[17] Once through the islands, the ship would lay about two miles off the beach at the edge of the shelving and launch the fuzileiros ashore in their rubber boats in the predawn twilight. Each

ship held 12 of the rubber boats and was capable of launching an entire DFE toward the shore. The boats were operated by members of the ship's landing party, who had been specially trained for the task at the Escola de Fuzileiros. The lead boat carried a radar reflector and would be guided by shipboard radar, with course corrections being relayed by radio. The landing was designed to put the fuzileiros ashore at daybreak, whereupon the rubber boats would return to the ship. Four or five days later, the ship would return from Porto Amélia, and the landing party would collect the fuzileiros and any prisoners.[18]

In the early phases of the war in Cabo Delgado, fuzileiros conducted operations on the Mueda Plain, where the enemy presence was most active. By March 1967, DFE 12 joined DFE 5 in Porto Amélia when the situation in Cabo Delgado deteriorated. The enemy in Cabo Delgado had numerous active groups that were well trained, well-armed and well led. Further, these groups had established internal sanctuaries that enabled them to move about with considerable security.

In June 1967, during Operation '*Teimosia*' ('Persistence'), DFE 12 was moving as an autonomous column in the direction of Chai (a village located about 20 miles from the coast) when it successfully located and assaulted an enemy encampment base: Pemba. With actions such as this, little by little the fuzileiros gained traction in Cabo Delgado; however, it was the population that suffered. The fuzileiros worked to bring security to the region south of Mocímboa da Praia during the dry season of 1967, a season that saw extremely difficult operations.[19]

As the autonomous columns ranged further and further from the coast, the risk to them rose. It was inglorious and dangerous work. In August 1967, recently-arrived DFE 1 conducted an offensive against the FRELIMO bases of Inhambane and Gaza.[20] FRELIMO base names bore no relation to their location, and indeed these two were in the Mueda Plain. The fuzileiros located one base while remaining undetected and approached it at about 0430 hours for a dawn attack. The approaches were known to be mined and booby-trapped, so some light was necessary to identify and avoid the explosives. As the fuzileiros assaulted and entered the compound, they discovered a partially-completed base with 30 huts ready for occupation, 20 under construction and indeed a rather permanent one of limestone, all of which were destroyed.

In operating in their assigned areas where FRELIMO had subverted the population, such as the North-East Mocímboa da Praia-Mueda Plain, the use of guides became a fundamental necessity. This was particularly true in areas where the cartography was weak and the distances great. The guides were vital because they were loyal, understood the terrain and spoke Portuguese.[21]

Throughout 1968, activity in Cabo Delgado remained intense and would continue because of its proximity to Tanzania, its easy access and its subverted population. The fuzileiros continued their patrols of the littoral, which was dangerous and tedious work. Nevertheless, there was a certain satisfaction in the fact that FRELIMO remained stalemated in Cabo Delgado for the remainder of the war and restricted to its north-east corner defined by a relatively straight line that ran from the frontier post of Negomano to the coastal town of Quissanga.[22]

(Endnotes)

1.   António José Telo, *Historia da Marinha Portuguesa: Homens, Doutrinas e Organização, 1824–1974* (Tomo I) [History of the Portuguese Navy: Men, Douctrine and Organization, 1824–1974 (Volume I) (Lisbon: Academia de Marinha, 1999), p.612.

2.   Neil Bruce, "Portugal's African Wars," *Conflict Studies*, ☐ 34 (March 1973), p.22.

3.   Al J. Venter, *The Zambesi Salient: Conflict in Southern Africa* (Cape Town: Howard Timmins, 1974), p.8.

4.   Abel Barroso Hipólito, *A Pacificação do Niassa: Um Caso Concreto de Contraguerrilha* [The Pacification of Niassa: A Concrete Case of Counterguerrilla War] (Lisbon: privately published, 1970), p.38.

5.   Telo, *Historia da Marinha Portuguesa*, p.609.

6.   Raúl Patrício Leitão, *O Quarto da Alva* [Morning Watch] (Lisbon: Âncora editor, 2012), pp.18–19.

7.   Delmar Barreiros, "Cobué: A zona mais pachola…" [Cobué: The prouder zone…], *Revista da Armada* (November 1984), pp.16–17.

8.   José Deolindo Torres Sobral and Raul Patrício Leitão, interview with the author, 10 April 2000, Lisbon.

9.   Torres Sobral and Leitão, interview.

10. Luís Sanches de Baêna, *Fuzileiros, Factos e Feitos na Guerrs de África 1961/1974: Crónica dos Feitos de Moçambique, Vol. IV* [Fuzileiros, Facts and Feats in the African War 1961/1974: Chronicle of Feats in Mozambique, Vol. IV] (Lisbon: Comissão Cultural da Marinha, 2006), p.50.

11. Ibid., p.59.

12. Ibid., p.48.

13. Leitão, *O Quarto da Alva*, pp.18–19.

14. 'Sepoy' is a term originally applied to a native of India in the military service of a European nation, and in its most common application, was used in the British Indian Army to describe an infantry private. Leitão in this case used the term to identify an African private in the Portuguese Navy. 'Sepoy' today remains a rank equivalent to Private in the armies of India, Pakistan and Bangladesh.

15. Baêna, *Fuzileiros*, vol. IV, p.131.

16. Adelino Rodrigues da Costa, *As Ilhas Quirimbas* [The Quirimbas Islands] (Lisbon: Edições Culturais da Marinha, 2003), p.86.

17. Ibid., p.92.

18. João Ferreira Barbosa, editing notes, 17 June 2011, Lisbon. Vice Admiral Ferreira Barbosa served as a junior officer on the FF *Vasco da Gama* (F478) patrolling the coast of Mozambique, 1967 to 1968.

19. Baêna, *Fuzileiros*, vol. IV, p.68.

20. Ibid., p.71.

21. Ibid., p.76.

22. Ibid., p.123.

CHAPTER 5
EAST OF ANGOLA

From 1965 onward, the navy moved east in Angola and brought river security similar to its success on the Zaire. There were four primary such systems in Eastern Angola, and these were the Zambezi, Cuando, Cuito and Cubango. All of these either provided a natural obstacle to maneuver, or an avenue of approach in that the insurgents either had to cross them or follow their courses to penetrate into the interior where there were worthy targets. For the Portuguese, they would serve as avenues of approach for combat and transport lines of communication for logistic operations. The fuzileiros would seek to control these systems and the commerce on them. It would also seek to engage the population on the littorals and be a positive influence on the economic and political landscape to counter insurgent proselytizing. As in Mozambique, the distant and remote river systems would be populated with launches and fuzileiros.

The navy opened its eastern offensive on 22 April 1966 with the deployment of a combat group from DFE 13 and its six rubber boats to Lungué-Bungo.[1] This was a spartan base created in the bush some 200 kilometers south-east of Luso on the road between Lucusse and Luvuei next to the river of the same name, an important tributary of the Zambezi. The local terrain contained areas of dense vegetation,

other areas so completely flooded that it was almost impossible to follow the course of the river, and still others that were totally deserted. This difficult terrain was periodically interrupted by the symmetry of a tilled field of crops, an ordinary cluster of huts and perhaps a small enemy encampment.[2]

The source of the Lungué-Bungo, like that of the Cuito, lay in the elevated region just south of Munhango or about 150 kilometers south-west of Luso. The river meandered for upwards of 2,000 kilometers before crossing the frontier with Zambia to join the Zambezi. It moved at a relentless seven knots through distant and isolated regions of extensive swamp forests and dense elephant grass.

The fuzileiros were quick to establish a nearly constant riverine presence with the mobility of their rubber boats and to engage and befriend the local people to gain their confidence. At the time, this part of Angola was about as remote from the influences of modern civilization as one could imagine, and in the first year of fuzileiro deployment, the war seemed very distant.[3] Soon afterwards though it became a hotbed of insurgent activity, and the navy and its fuzileiros expanded their presence in this remoteness to establish a successful offensive against the enemy penetration from Zambia.

A rubber boat with its fuzileiros on patrol along the Cuito River near the Zambian border. (Source: Escola de Fuzileiros)

The Insurgent Problem

In April 1966, following an intense effort to proselytize the population in the east, first in the district of Moxico and later in Cuando-Cubango, the MPLA infiltrated a large group of combatants into the Cazombo Salient.[4] This is the large, approximately square geographical protrusion that is bounded by Zaire and Zambia on three sides and measures about 240 kilometers per side. It is crossed diagonally by the Zambezi, which ultimately flows through Zambia, over Victoria Falls and through Mozambique to the Indian Ocean. Because of its shape, exposed borders and remoteness, it was quite vulnerable to incursions. These infiltrated MPLA combatants showed a remarkable improvement over earlier Portuguese experience in subverting the population and employing selective terror when it did not cooperate. Subversion of the population in the east was estimated to be a modest 6 percent in 1965 and had grown to about 42 percent by 1968, the year that the MPLA offensive attained its height.[5]

In October 1966, following the penetration of the Cazombo Salient, there was a surge of activity to the south in the triangle bounded by the settlements of Ninda, Sete and Chiume. These were located next to the Zambian border and about 375 kilometers southeast of Luso in an area called *'Terras do Fim do Mundo'*, or 'Lands at the End of the Earth'. This area is more than 1,000 kilometers from the Atlantic Ocean, and the settlement of Luiana in the extreme southeast is equidistant from Luanda on the Atlantic and Beira on the Indian Ocean. It was this remoteness and the fact that the temperate savannah climate of Central Angola, as it spreads south into this area with its lower altitude, becomes so harsh and desiccated that it prompted this apt name. Such an operating environment favored the insurgent in that he was easily able to detect Portuguese forces at considerable distance and did so generally before they were aware of him. This insurgent advantage made it difficult for Portuguese forces to find and destroy the enemy, and as we shall see, substantially influenced the crafting of a campaign plan.

Action-Counteraction

The MPLA from its Zambian bases planned a two-pronged assault. The southern one would be mounted from Mungu, Shangombe and Sikongo, and known as the 'Route of the Cuando'. It would follow this river valley westward with the plan of reaching the populated and wealthy district of Bié and the central plain of Huambo: the heart of Angola. From this point the insurgents hoped to control the entire country and to reach all the way to Malange through an axis of advance along the Cuanza River Valley.[6] The northern one was called the 'Route of the Luena', or the 'Agostinho Neto Route' by the MPLA, and was to be launched from Chipango and Cassamba and aimed along this river directly at Luso – and from there to the highland plain of Malange. The hope was to gain control of the Luanda-Malange railway, reach Luanda and link with forces coming from the north.[7]

Campaign plans for the UPA/FNLA are much less distinct. Its plan can be imputed from the attempt in 1970 to infiltrate three battalions in the north with the goal of controlling the rich, coffee-growing region north of the Luanda-Malange railway and paralyzing the Angolan economy, an objective that failed in 1961. This offensive action would bring its forces to the gates of Luanda and precipitate a sudden conclusion to the conflict. The offensive was abandoned in September 1972 because it was isolated logistically deep in Portuguese territory, besieged by both the MPLA and the Portuguese, and thus stood little chance of success. UNITA simply intended to establish a base deep in the interior of Angola, and using some notion of the *tâche d'huile* theory of expanding control, mobilize an ever-increasing number of the population to gain the 'total independence of Angola'.

The need for this lengthy approach was prompted by a number of factors: first, Portugal had limited manpower to police the vast region of the east. This limitation dictated an approach that enlisted the sparse terrain, geographic remoteness and harsh climate as allies in isolating the insurgents in an attritional war; second, these three regional characteristics appeared to favor the insurgent in that he could easily

Fuzileiros make a landing to patrol inland along the banks of the Cuito River. (Source: Escola de Fuzileiros)

hide or move largely unhindered by Portuguese forces. Consequently, with a containment strategy in which Portuguese forces would define and then gradually reduce the area of insurgent contamination, the enemy would be forced to fight from a progressively reduced and isolated position and be ultimately destroyed. The few local people living in the east and south-east could hardly subsist themselves – much less support the insurgents with food, recruits, intelligence and shelter. In summary, Portuguese theater strategy was based on sound reasoning following a considered appraisal of opponent strengths, battlefield terrain and resident population.

Conversely, the several insurgent organizations based their strategies on the hope that the population would welcome them or acquiesce, and that Portuguese forces could be overcome. This approach required a leap of faith from a population experiencing unprecedented material gains, an unlikely event. While the insurgents were skilled fighters, they chose a battlefield in which Portuguese mobility could easily outflank and reduce their foot soldiers over time in what would become a universally hostile environment. Lastly, the Portuguese strategy was designed to wear the enemy both psychologically and physically, and to reinforce the notion in his mind of the substantial cost in treasure, time and lives without commensurate gain. Ultimately, at the national level it was aimed at convincing Portuguese adversaries that their political objective was neither attainable, or not worth the apparent cost.

Naval Force Projection

While the navy had earlier augmented its presence on the disparate waters of the Cuanza on the Atlantic, the Zaire in the north, and on the Chiloango and Lake Massábi in Cabinda, it was now called to support and help secure the population of the south, south-east and east. To this end it established a presence at four sites on key rivers: Lungué-Bungo on the river of the same name, Chilombo and Lumbala on the Zambezi, Rivungo on the Cuando and Vila Nova da Armada at the confluences of the Cuito, Longa and Cato Rivers. This naval augmentation of the east was facilitated by the closing of certain posts on the Zaire and the consequent consolidation, reduction and transfer of forces.

Fuzileiro deployment to the Lungué-Bungo began on 22 April 1966, although initial planning had begun the preceding month. At first the fuzileiro base was located next to the raft ferry crossing on the primitive road between Lucusse and Luvuei. This was short-lived, however, as the navy began moving it in August to a site about 30 kilometers upstream and west to the bridge that carried the improved road between Lucusse and Luzi. This move was completed within a week, and in September prefabricated wooden buildings were erected, as the force was augmented from combat groups to a full DFE. This base was important, as the Lungué-Bungo was directly in the path of a critical supply route for MPLA forces operating in the interior near the river headwaters. In executing its mission, the

Fuzileiros patrolling along the Zambezi River near Lumbala. (Source: Escola de Fuzileiros)

An LDP at a remote settlement in Eastern Angola maneuvering to land. (Source: Escola de Fuzileiros)

DFE was to coordinate with the army in interdicting the enemy, to befriend and support the local population along the river, and to gather intelligence. Personnel rotations between this and other sites were such that it is not useful to try to identify a particular DFE as being deployed to a specific site.

The Zambezi was the easternmost river in the path of the invading MPLA, and beginning on 18 November 1966, two combat groups of special fuzileiros were deployed to Lumbala with their rubber boats. On 14 October 1967, the groups were augmented to a DFE-sized force and moved again 30 kilometers north to the village of Chilombo. This site was located on the left bank of the Zambezi in the heart of the Cazombo Salient and more centrally in the area of Cazombo, Lumbala and Caripande, an extension of more than 100 miles. This extension proved to be navigable by LDP-sized launches during the months from January to June as a result of the rainy season, and consequently LDP 208 was identified to add support. The location at Chilombo put the fuzileiros in a position to challenge the advancing MPLA columns directly, and thus enemy contact was frequent and intense.

From 5 January, LDP 208 was used to patrol the Zambezi River between Cazumbo and Caripande. Eight days after commencing patrol operations, the launch and its fuzileiros were attacked from the riverbank at the confluence of the Zambezi and Calupemba by seven enemy using automatic weapons. Of the 13 fuzileiros on the launch, only one was lightly wounded. Five years would pass uneventfully before another incident, and in the meantime LDP 208 would perform its vital logistical support operations in an area bereft of roads.[8]

Additionally, the navy established a presence on the Cuando from 26 June 1967 with the arrival of LDP 210 in Eastern Angola. It was based at the settlement of Rivungo on the right bank of the river, which defines the frontier with Zambia in that area, and was located in the vicinity of Neriquinha and Luiana in the extreme south-east. This small presence on the remote, complex and lengthy river frontier proved difficult to support and presented a hardship on the small force of three sailors and five fuzileiros who manned the launch. The force was designated as the River Cuando Naval Detachment (*Destacamento de Marinha do rio Cuando*, or DESTACMAR-CUANDO).[9]

There was little navigational information on the Cuando, and thus patrols were based largely on aerial reconnaissance photographs. There were no charts or reliable maps of the area, and indeed it was a largely unknown region. The river had never been navigated by anything other than a canoe, and apparently no white man had been much seen in the area since Serpa Pinto had conducted his expeditions to the Zambezi Basin in 1869 and 1877. The river current was only two to three knots, but the river itself wound its way through many meanders and switchbacks with their myriad branches. This sinuous characteristic made patrolling a long and tedious process. The length of a patrol between the Caprivi Strip and the upper reaches of the Cuando was approximately a 940-mile round trip because of the wandering nature of the river and took between 12 and 13 days depending on what was encountered. A patrol required about 135 hours of navigation, but it could only be done in the daylight, and air support in the form of a T-6 Harvard from Gago Coutinho was indispensable. Fuel and supplies were difficult to obtain in such remoteness where there was a single army post and no other government presence. This meager logistic support was supplemented by hunting, as the area was full of game. The MPLA was supposed to be in the area, as this river was its 'Route of the Cuando'; however, the insurgents were not seen often. When they were encountered, the crew responded with heavy fire, and the insurgents vanished.[10]

On 23 July 1969, there was an incident in which the launch was attacked from the high grass opposite Mungulhi with machine gun fire, which was returned by fire from the Oerlinkon and two MG-42s. The launch maneuvered for two hours to fix the enemy and hold him in place until air support could arrive. The intimidating effect of the heavy Oerlinkon kept the enemy at bay, and while his casualties were unknown, the superior firepower of the launch over that of the insurgents was an effective deterrent. From the point of view of the insurgents, the river patrol was to be avoided as a needless impediment, for their primary target was the population further inland to the north-west. Small groups of insurgents traveling light would be little match for a heavily-armed force and would be relying on the vastness of the 'Terras do Fim do Mundo' to hide and avoid Portuguese land and naval patrols during their transit.

Vila Nova da Armada, the most important of the eastern river posts, was established on the Cuito River on 31 July 1968 when LDP 105 arrived. The Cuito was navigable from Cuito Cuanavale as far as Quedas da M'Pupa, the dramatic rapids some 400 miles downstream past Riabela, Vila Nova da Armada, Rito and Maue, or Mané.[11] The site of Vila Nova da Armada was in the district of Cuando-Cubango on the right bank of the river and between the confluences of the Cuito and the Longa to the north and the Cuito and the Cato to the south. Cuito Cuanavale, Baixo-Longa, Longa and the more distant Serpa Pinto were neighboring towns. By that December, the base had a platoon of special fuzileiros and by March 1969, a company of naval fuzileiros (CF 3). The construction of permanent buildings was begun in February 1969 and concluded in December 1970. Included in these improvements were electrification, a 2,200-meter airstrip, supply warehouses, magazines, repair shops, messing facilities and living quarters.[12] Cuito Cuanavale became the Naval Detachment Cuito (*Destacamento de Marinha do rio Cuito*, or DESTACMAR-CUITO).[13]

In 1973, CF 3 consisted of six officers, 15 sergeants and 31 fuzileiros, and these were divided into three platoons. The unit was responsible for an immense area of 37,000 square kilometers, which was greater than the Alentejo region of the *metrópole*. The normal fuzileiro assignment was the routine patrol of the river and its tributaries in the ubiquitous rubber boats, but in 1973 – the year that the campaign in the east was effectively concluded – there were some 19 actions and operations, or about one every 19 days.[14] During these 19 events, the fuzileiros accounted for 50 enemy dead and the destruction of four encampments.[15] In an operating area of this magnitude, finding four enemy camps was a noteworthy feat in itself. Probably the most important accomplishment of CF 3, however, was within its own backyard, where it established a school for the neighboring population; assisted in the improvement of local hygiene and sanitation practices; ran a transportation system along the river; and assisted in the construction of nearby houses and villages.[16] This widespread mobilization of the population to effect economic recovery – and hence indispensable social stabilization – yielded a victory over the insurgent movements that was almost unheralded. In an interview with the journalist José Freire Antunes following the war, Daniel Chipenda of the MPLA remarked that the Portuguese had succeeded in protecting the population and had prevented the MPLA from delivering on its promises of a better life. More importantly, the population was united in understanding that the Portuguese offered a better choice.[17] The fuzileiros made an indispensable contribution to this victory.

The remote area in the southeast of Angola, the 'Lands of the End of the Earth' as it was known, became a transit area between Zambia and the Caprivi Strip for SWAPO insurgents from September 1965 onward. To bring security to the vast area, the Portuguese Navy established a number of river outposts manned by fuzileiros to counter enemy use of the rivers as navigational aids and to protect the local population from the predations of the insurgents. When the fuzileiros established Vila Nova da Armada in July 1968, it was indeed an outpost in the classic sense with its several tents and a straw hut for messing and headquarters, as one of the fuzileiros captured with his camera. Over the year 1970, these temporary structures were replaced with permanent ones. (Source: José António Rodrigues Pereira)

(Endnotes)

1. Freire da Cruz Júnior, "Evolução das Infra-estruturas da Armada no Ultramar" [Evolution of Naval Infrastructure in the *Ultramar*], in the unpublished collection *Participação da Armada na Defesa das Províncias Ultramarinas* [Participation of the Navy in the Defense of the Overseas Provinces], TMs [photocopy], 1972, p.17.

2. A. Pimentel Saraiva, "Postais do Ultramar: Angola – Postal № 2, Luanda, Zaire, Cabinda e Leste de Angola" [Overseas Postcards: Angola – Postcard № 2, Luanda, Zaire, Cabinda and the East of Angola], *Anais do Clube Militar Naval* (April/June 1968), p.312.

3. Manuel Pinto Machado, "Postais do Ultramar: Angola – Postal № 3, Lungué-Bungo fins do octobro 68" [Overseas Postcards: Angola – Postcard № 3, Lungué-Bungo End of October '68], *Anais do Clube Militar Naval* (October/December 1968), pp.695–696.

4. António Pires Nunes, *Angola 1966–1974, Vitória Militar no Leste* [Angola 1966–1974, Military Victory in the East] (Lisbon: Prefácio, 2002), p.21.

5. Ibid., p.6.

6. Ibid., p.40.

7. Ibid.

8. Ibid.

9. Ibid.

10. António Luís Marinho de Castro, interview by the author, 30 January 2003, Lisbon.

11. José Alberto Lopes Carvalheira, "Acção da Marinha em Águas Interiores (1961–1971)" [Naval Operations in Inland Waters (1961–1971)], in the unpublished collection *Participação da Armada na Defesa das Províncias Ultramarinas* [Participation of the Navy in the Defense of the Overseas Provinces], TMs [photocopy], 1972, p.34

12. Cruz Júnior, "Evolução das Infra-estructuras da Armada no Ultramar", pp.19–20.

13. Lopes Carvalheira, "Acção da Marinha em Águas Interiores (1961–1971)", p.34.

14. António José Telo, *História da Marinha Portuguesa: Homens, Doutrinas e Organização, 1824–1974* (Tomo I) [History of the Portuguese Navy: Men, Doctrine and Organization, 1824–1974 (Volume I)] (Lisbon: Academia de Marinha, 1999), p.605. The difference between an action and an operation was that an action used two or less combat groups, while an operation used more than two.

15. Ibid.

16. Ibid.

17. José Freire Antunes, *A Guerra de África 1961–1974* [The War of Africa 1961–1974] (Lisbon: Temas e Debates, 1996), p.851.

CHAPTER 6
THE COST

For 13 years, Portugal was confronted by an international community manifestly hostile to its presence in Africa and committed to oppose it by all means available. Ignored in this hostility were the centuries of Portuguese presence in these African regions and the Portuguese efforts to bring to them advances in education, healthcare and economic prosperity. In 1961, Portugal found itself in a fight to retain its African possessions that extended from the Atlantic to the Indian Ocean, to both sides of the equator and to thousands of square miles of vast and difficult terrain. This campaign represented one of the largest combat fronts in modern history. The logistics of training, deploying and supplying forces to fight on such an expansive battlefield was staggering. The fuzileiro units – scattered across the rivers, lakes and narrow seas of Africa, enduring the hardships of isolation in the bush and the confines of the great and small launches – fought a noble action: one that is today little remembered. For them, this was a war not lost on the field of battle.

The fuzileiros, reborn under the lucid vision of Admiral Roboredo e Silva, conducted themselves in extemporary fashion – adhering to their centuries-old heritage – and left the continent with their heads held high. A total of 154 fuzileiros gave their lives in Africa. Fuzileiro heroism is remarkable for the small force: four Orders of the Tower and Sword, 12 Medals of Military Valor with Palm, 156 War Cross Medals and 49 Medals of Military Service with Distinction with Palm.

The fuzileiros today proudly continue their tradition as the Special Operations Force of the Portuguese Navy. The *Corpo de Fuzileiros* now numbers about 1,450 – down from a wartime high of 3,400 – and is organized into seven operational units: the 1st and 2nd Battalions of Fuzileiros, the Amphibious Unit, the Naval Policing Unit, the Special Operations Detachment, the Fire Support Company and the Tactical Transport Support Company. The corps retains its specializations in amphibious warfare, coastal reconnaissance, unconventional warfare, guerrilla warfare, raids, maritime interdiction and boarding operations – as well as remaining an elite light infantry force with a rapid reaction capability.

Fuzileiros today, as in Alpoim Calvão's time, must undergo one of the longest and most physically demanding specialist infantry training regimes in the world – lasting some 42 weeks. The mud bowl still exists at the Vale de Zebro, and perhaps only 15 percent to 35 percent of the inductees eventually pass the course and are awarded their traditional (and highly coveted) navy blue beret. The traditions of excellence remain, as well as those of ceremony, for the fuzileiros – with their singular privilege – are always to the right in any military formation and break ranks ahead of all others, as it has been for their centuries-old history.

Table 6
Fuzileiro Deaths in Africa, 1962–1975

	Combat	Accident in Combat	Accident in Service	Accident not in Service	Sickness	Total
Angola	12	1	23	5	2	43
Guiné	50	8	16	7	5	86
Mozambique	12	1	2	7	1	23
Cape Verde			1	1		2
Total	74	10	42	20	8	154

Source: Luís Sanches de Baêna, *Fuzileiros, Factos e Feitos na Guerra de África, 1961–1974, Vol. 1* [Fuzileiros, Facts and Feats in the African War, 1961/1974, Vol. 1] (Lisbon: Comissão Cultural da Marinha, 2006), p.87.

Bibliography

Afonso, Aniceto and Carlos de Matos Gomes, *Guerra Colonial* [Colonial War] (Lisbon: Notícias, 2000).

Antunes, José Freire, *A Guerra de África 1961–1974* [The War of Africa 1961–1974] (Lisbon: Temas e Debates, 1996).

Baêna, Luís Sanches de, *Fuzileiros: Factos e Feitos na Guerra de África 1961/1974* [Fuzileiros: Facts and Feats in the African War 1961/1974] (Lisbon: Comissão Cultural da Marinha, 2006).

Calvão, Guilherme Almor de Alpoim, *De Conakry ao M.D.L.P.* [From Conakry to the M.D.L.P.] (Lisbon: Editorial Intervenção, 1976).

Costa, Adelino Rodrigues da, *As Ilhas Quirimbas* [The Quirimbas Islands] (Lisbon: Edições Culturais da Marinha, 2003).

Hortelão, Rui, Luís Sanches de and Abel Melo e Sousa, *Alpoim Calvão, Honra e Dever* [Alpoim Calvão, Honor and Duty] (Porto: Caminhos Romanos, 2012).

Leitão, Raúl Patrício, *O Quarto da Alva* [Morning Watch] (Lisbon: Âncora editor, 2012).

Nunes, António Pires, *Angola 1966–1974, Vitória Militar no Leste* [Angola 1966–1974, Military Victory in the East] (Lisbon: Prefácio, 2002).

Talhadas, José, *Memórias de um guerreiro colonial* [Memories of a colonial warrior] (Lisbon: Ancora, 2010).

Van der Waals, Willem S., *Portugal's War in Angola 1961–1974* (Rivonia: Ashanti Publishing, 1993).

Venter, Al J., *Portugal's Insurgent War, The Campaign for Africa* (Cape Town: John Malherbe, 1973).

_____ *The Zambesi Salient: Conflict in Southern Africa* (Cape Town: Howard Timmins, 1974).

Acknowledgments

This book is the story of the fuzileiros, or Portuguese Marines, in Africa between 1961 and 1974 – and as such would not have been possible without the unstinting support of my dear friend Admiral Nuno Gonçalo Vieira Matias: a former Chief of Staff of the Portuguese Navy, a veteran of Africa and a fuzileiro himself. His support in developing access to the needed photographs and references was indispensable. Additionally I owe a debt of gratitude to the *Corpo de Fuzileiros*: its Commander, Rear Admiral Luís Carlos de Sousa Pereira, and its Deputy Commander, Captain Carlos Teixeira Moreira, for their extensive support.

The generous time afforded me for interviews by Captain Guilherme Almor de Alpoim Calvão over many years likewise helped me to develop a personal feel for the fuzileiro culture and was deeply appreciated. Similarly the time spent with Raul Patrício Leitão added an indispensable understanding to operations and life on Lake Niassa. The correspondence with José de Conceição Gomes Talhadas again completed another perspective on fuzileiro life in the African combat environment and is deeply valued. I am also indebted to *Comandantes* José Manuel Malhão Pereira, Paulo Lownes Marques, Vasco Quevedo Pessanha and Carlos Encaração Gomes, and am most grateful for the time that they took to share their observations over the years.

Finally, I owe particular debt to my wife Anne, who lived patiently with the domestic chaos of this work.

About the author

John P. Cann is a Research Fellow and retired Professor of National Security Studies at Marine Corps University, a former member of the research staff at the Institute for Defense Analyses, and former Scholar-in-Residence at the University of Virginia. He earned his Doctorate in War Studies at King's College London in 1996, published *Counterinsurgency in Africa* in 1997, *Memories of Portugal's African Wars, 1961–1975* (ed.) in 1998, *The Brown Waters of Africa* in 2008, *The Flechas* in 2013, *Flight Plan Africa* in 2015 and some 30 plus articles on small wars over the years. He is a retired naval captain and flight officer specializing in open ocean reconnaissance aviation and served in a variety of aviation assignments, including command. He has been awarded the Portuguese Navy Cross Medal and the Medal of Dom Afonso Henriques for his writings on conflict in Lusophone Africa, and is an Associate Member of the Academia de Marinha.